IMPOSSIBLE
MOTHERHOOD

ALSO BY IRENE VILAR

The Ladies' Gallery

IMPOSSIBLE
MOTHERHOOD
Testimony *of an* Abortion Addict

IRENE VILAR

Foreword by Robin Morgan

Other Press
New York

Production Editor: Yvonne E. Cárdenas

Book design: Simon M. Sullivan

This book was set in 11 pt Garamond by
Alpha Design & Composition of Pittsfield, NH.

Epigraph on page vii translated by A. J. Krailsheimer
(New York: Penguin, 1995)

10 9 8 7 6 5 4 3 2 1

A portion of the proceeds from the sale of this book will go to
The Sisterhood is Global Institute (www.sigi.org)

sisterhood is gl bal
institute

Library of Congress Cataloging-in-Publication Data

Vilar, Irene, 1969–
Impossible motherhood : testimony of an abortion addict /
Irene Vilar ; foreword by Robin Morgan.
p. cm.
ISBN 978-1-59051-320-0 (pbk.) — ISBN 978-1-59051-363-
7 (e-book) 1. Vilar, Irene, 1969– 2. Abortion—
Psychological aspects—Case studies. 3. Compulsive
behavior—Case studies. 4. College teachers' spouses—
Biography. I. Title.
HQ767.V55 2009
616.85'84—dc22
[B]
2009012880

This memoir is a true story. However, certain names and
identifying characteristics have been changed to protect the
privacy of the individuals portrayed in this book. The author has
also reconstructed conversations to the best of her recollection.

To Dan

Evil is easy, its forms are infinite; good is almost unique. But there is a kind of evil as difficult to identify as what is called good, and often this particular evil passes for good because of this trait. Indeed one needs an extraordinary greatness of soul to attain it as much as to attain good.

PASCAL, *Pensées*

FOREWORD
Robin Morgan

Irene Vilar had fifteen abortions in fifteen years. These pages chart her course to discover why—a search that defies stereotypes we were certain we had long relinquished.

First, it should be noted that Vilar can *write* (unfortunately not a given in authors these days). Consequently, this memoir reads as hauntingly as an Isabelle Allende novel—but here the Latin American genre of magical realism is brutally true. These pages expose intricate, intimate nuances of female suffering, survival, and self-reclamation in complex terms that, as Vilar notes, won't fit on a bumper sticker.

Second, Vilar is a pro-choice feminist who for years refused to write this book from understandable fear that she might be misunderstood and, worse, that her story might compromise women's reproductive right to choose. She even wrote an earlier, self-censoring memoir, *The Ladies' Gallery*, wherein the "horror script I lived out with the man I loved and became pregnant by multiple times . . . is absent."

Third, Vilar is a Latina, a Puerto Rican American, and therein lies a tale of colonialism compounding sexism. As she writes, "Latin America holds some of the world's most stringent abortion laws, yet it still has the world's highest rate of abortions . . . many repeat abortions. It becomes unsustainable to identify at any level with the 'pro-life' movement when it fundamentally calls for the

United States to regress to Latin America's horrific abortion and women mortality figures and ignores Western Europe's impressive low abortion statistics."

Vilar's story unfurls against densely layered backdrops: patriarchy in the home and the state, racism, colonialism and neocolonialism, and a "tradition" of secrecy about sexual abuse of girls by male relatives.

It begins with a larger-than-life grandmother, forced to sell herself for rent at age seventeen, leaving Puerto Rico to seek survival in New York's sweatshop factories. Her fierce commitment to the Puerto Rican Nationalist movement culminated in 1954, when she raced up the U.S. Capitol's steps with a gun and a national flag in her purse. This woman, Lolita Lebrón—famous or infamous, depending on political perspective—served twenty-seven years in prison for "attempting to overthrow the government of the United States." Decades later, still militant at age eighty-four, she was imprisoned yet again for protesting the U.S. Navy's presence in Vieques. Lebrón was a heroic figure, but her chosen sacrifice also required "public mythmaking" that cost her family—especially the women—dearly.

Lebrón's daughter grew up with a sexually abusive uncle and sought refuge in marriage at age fifteen, forging for herself "pleasure in making a show of servility." She became a Valium addict who attempted suicide—finally succeeding at it by throwing herself out of a moving car when her daughter, Irene, our author, was only eight. Meanwhile, Vilar's father was addicted to alcohol and gambling, and two of her three brothers were heroin addicts, one dying of an overdose. It's mildly miraculous that Irene Vilar is vertical at all.

Context is crucial. She writes, "I can't think about my mother and in general Puerto Rican women without thinking about 'choice' . . . [a word that] invokes free will based on individual freedom, obscuring the dynamics between social constraints and human activity. . . . While population growth has been blamed for Puerto Rico's widespread poverty, other causes, such as American exploitation, were ignored or covered up. The 1967 NBA winner for nonfiction, *La Vida* by Oscar Lewis, reiterated the views of U.S. social scientists in turning fertility and reproduction into the source of the 'Puerto Rican problem.' The Puerto Rican mother was either victimized by her macho husand and countless children, longing to be rescued from her own ignorance, or a relentless mating machine that needed to be stopped."

Vilar is tragically accurate. From 1955 to 1969, Puerto Rico was a U.S. government laboratory testing female contraceptives, in particular high-dosage pills with hazardous side effects that included sterility. I remember demonstrating with other young feminist activists against the use of Puerto Rican women as contraceptive "guinea pigs." That was in 1968, when women in Puerto Rico were more than ten times likely to be sterilized than were women in the U.S. *By 1974, 37 percent of Puerto Rican women of childbearing age had been permanently sterilized.* By 1980, Puerto Rico had the highest per-capita rate of sterilization on the planet.

Vilar's mother was sixteen when she first gave birth, in January 1956, followed that October by a six-month preemie. She used a controversial birth-control pill, but in 1961, after another birth, the public hospital refused care if she didn't consent to tubal ligation. Eight years later, her tubes became untied and Irene was conceived. When a doctor recommended a hysterectomy, this woman was sent home with no reproductive system *and* no hormonal treatment—at age thirty-three. Vilar sums up the result: "What growing up poor and an orphan, the daughter of a woman imprisoned in the U.S., and the wife for twenty-three years of a man unable to value her could not do, the U.S. mass sterilization program and its racist population control ideologies did. . . . [My] mother came undone while I watched."

Watching, the child learned multiple, conflicting lessons, becoming more confused once denial set in with familial familiarity. Even decades later, Lebrón railed at her granddaughter's desire to write the truth: "[M]y family is the nation of Puerto Rico to which I have given my life, and you listen well, anyone who threatens the nation is the enemy . . . saying Tatita did not die in a car accident but killed herself . . . You publish that book and the movement won't forgive you. . . . I *am* the Movement!"

So what happened to that bright, eight-year-old little girl who watched her mother lose her mind and then, deliberately, her life?

Determined to rise above grief, yet clinging to her inheritance— the disease to please—she earned straight A's in seven schools in seven years and entered college at fifteen. So far, she had changed the trajectory of tragedy via her intellect, not her body. But the past catches up to that intelligent, passionate, young woman trying to negotiate between deprivation and education, false liberties and real freedom. And patriarchy whispers to that hungry intellect that there is only one way to feed it.

She can never herself become the brilliant Great Woman she longs to be. She must find a Great Man, a Pygmalion, a Svengali, a lover-tutor-father figure to whom she can surrender herself, through whom she can bloom. At age sixteen, Irene found her Great Man, age fifty. During her decade in his thrall she endured multiple abortions and suicide attempts, and hospitalization in a mental ward.

Ah yes, the Great Man.

These days, the feminist prophecy "We are becoming the men we wanted to marry" is actually true. But until quite recently, educated, intellectual, otherwise strong young women—especially though not exclusively artists and writers—were particular prey for Great Men. We went nervously but willingly; so accustomed were we to superimposing ghosts of ourselves into the generic He's, Him's, and Mankinds; so reconciled to seeking anything resembling our alternate realities between the lines of theirs—for their reality was almost always one in which female human beings were absent, offstage, and one- or two-dimensional. Worse, we stuck it out, validating the very lies we'd been taught about "inherent female masochism." We rejected identifying with other women (even many lesbians did so: Gertrude Stein, Elizabeth Bishop), because only men were fully human, only men possessed the agency to act on life. Each of us desperate to be the "exceptional" woman in her Great Man's judgmental eyes strained for power, for voice itself, through *him*.

When we had served his purpose—adoring student, muse, mate, mommy, sex toy, breadwinner (so he could work at his *art*), harpy (if we rebelled)—he destroyed us. Some women—Sylvia Plath and Anne Sexton among them—gave him the convenience of their suicide. Some of us managed to escape. I was one such woman— but it took me twenty years to break free. So I don't dismiss Vilar's predicament lightly.

Her Great Man was one of her teachers, a professor of Latin American Literature and Theory who boasted friendships with such Other Great Men as Julio Cortázar, Carlos Fuentes, Gabriel García Márquez, Manuel Puig, and Octavio Paz (that list alone could serve as a warning to spirited women). An Argentinean Jew, atheist philosopher, survivor of a generation jailed and murdered under dictatorship, he was a rebel. Vilar's rebellion, not permitted to her directly, could be manifest via him.

He positioned their relationship as her salvation, on his terms— a permanent audition. He told her his lovers never lasted more than five years, that family kills desire, that he'd fought to stay fatherless, that previous companions couldn't bear the price of a life in freedom. He told her mature, less pliable women were riddled with worries and wounds. Amazingly, he admitted flat out, "I need an unformed woman, unfinished, with not too many wounds. That's why I like young women."

The sole rebellion Irene Vilar *could* manage was to "forget" to take her birth control pills (redolent anyway of cultural and family humiliation)—and get pregnant. *With each pregnancy she defied him.* But to *keep* the lifeline he represented, it was then imperative to become *un*pregnant. So was the cycle established.

Meanwhile, she devoured writing by men he prescribed. Cortázar, Fuentes, Fernández, Bertrand Russel, Martin Buber, and especially theologian Paul Tillich, whom she read when pregnant the first time. Tillich's influence runs through her book, in her quest for what he termed "the courage to be."

So it's worthwhile pausing briefly to examine the alternate reality regarding that particular Great Man, revealed to us with compassionate but uncompromising honesty by his widow, Hannah Tillich, in her book, *From Time to Time* (Chelsea, MI; Scarborough House, 1973). After his death, she tells us, she "unlocked the drawers." There was the pornographic letter hidden under his blotter; the revelation of his favorite fantasy of naked women, *crucified*, being whipped; the discovery of all the photos, affairs, mistresses, sexual secretaries, one-night stands, the abuse of worshipful female students. Hannah Tillich writes, "I was tempted to place between the sacred pages of his highly esteemed lifework these obscene signs of the real life that he had transformed into the gold of abstraction—King Midas of the spirit." Instead, Hannah Tillich dared write this book alchemizing her own integrity out of "the piece of bleeding, tortured womanhood" she writes she had become.

So dares Vilar—who insists on taking principled responsibility for her own actions, even while contextualizing them: in one eight-month period, she was "responsible" for an affair, a suicide attempt, three car accidents, two boat collisions, and two abortions. Her weight dropped to ninety-five pounds—at five foot six. "Each time I got my period, I was sad. Each time I discovered I was pregnant, I was aroused and afraid." But Vilar finally noticed that when she began to write seriously—in those "moments of creativity and validation, I evaded the drama of pregnancy and abortion and 'remembered' to take my birth control pills." My, what a coincidence.

While reading this book, I kept wondering where was the Women's Movement as a support/sanity making/survival factor in Vilar's life—as it has been for the past 40 years in so many millions of women's lives? How did we fail her? We know that there are countries where access to contraception is so drastically limited that women are forced into multiple abortions as a method of birth control, but that was not the case here. Was her addiction so deep or his spell so strong that she avoided the visible, available feminist groups on campus, in the cities and towns where she lived? Or did some feminists, trapped in an ethnocentric myopia of our own as "gringas," fail to reach out meaningfully so that *all* the intersecting factors in her suffering, including racism and colonialism, could be addressed?

Vilar did have close women friends, but they seemed unable or unwilling to exert sufficient counterbalance to the Great Man—nor did she always allow them into the full truths about her life. Yet a major shift occurred on reading Simone de Beauvoir's *Memoirs of a Dutiful Daughter*, "which shook me profoundly about the intimate picture of a young woman growing up aground in a suffocating world and striking out on her own with such existential ambition that even a mother's death becomes a footnote to her story." At last, Vilar dared admit she "felt cornered, obliged to choose between him and my life."

Then of course, to keep her, he plied the ultimate twist of the knife. He said she didn't have to have another abortion the next day. He said he was ready to "give" her a child if that's what she wanted. Irony begets irony. She found herself shocked to realize she didn't want his child.

In a 1974 essay, "On Women as a Colonized People" (collected in Morgan, *The Word of a Woman: Feminist Dispatches*, W.W. Norton), I analyzed how Franz Fanon and Albert Memmi had defined the characteristics of colonization: the oppressed are robbed of culture, history, pride, and their land itself, and are forced (by systemic punishment and reward) to adopt the oppressor's language, values, even identity. In time, they become alienated from their own values, even their land—which is being mined by the colonizer for its natural resources. The colonized are permitted (forced) to work the land, but not benefiting from what it produces, come to feel oppressed by it. Thus, alienation from their own territory serves to mystify that territory, and enforced identification with colonizing masters provokes eventual shame for themselves and contempt for their land. It follows that the first goal of a colonized people is to reclaim their land. What Fanon and Memmi never grasped was that *women per se are a colonized people*. Our history, values, voices, and (cross-cultural) culture have been taken from us—manifest in patriarchal seizure of our basic "land." Our own *bodies* have been taken from us, mined for their natural resources (sex, children, and labor), and alienated/mystified, whether as stereotypical virgin, whore, or mother. It follows that as women, to reclaim our lives we must reclaim our flesh.

Irene Vilar, multiply colonized, reclaimed her life when she finally brought to term and birthed the woman she is today, after so many decades of a tragedy infinitely worse than all her pregnancy terminations: *the aborted self.* Those who think the struggle for women's freedom and power no longer necessary or single-issue simplistic would do well to read this book. We dare not forget that a woman's right to control her own body includes not just the right to control her womb but also her *voice*. Irene Vilar has courageously let that voice sing. Listen to it.

Robin Morgan
New York City
March 8, 2009

PROLOGUE

My life could be summed up by the extreme human experience of abortion. For years, reading or hearing about an abortion immediately turned the words into a maelstrom of emotions. Every time I came upon the song by America "A Horse with No Name" or the book *The Last of the Just*, which accompanied me during a shameful decade of my life, I was deeply upset.

It is not a comfortable thought to contemplate the morality of my actions. The moral issue of abortion is a difficult one, I think, because it is unusual. And it is unusual because the human fetus is so unlike anything or anyone else, and because the relationship between the fetus and the pregnant woman is so unique, so unlike any other relationship.

I began this book in 2001 as the Pygmalion/My Fair Lady story of an older man and a teenager, a teacher and a student, and the predictable but not uninteresting dissolution of their mutual fascination. But this changed. The story that needed to be told was that of an addiction. Despite my efforts to fight it, I became obsessed with the idea. Following through with the book seemed a terrifying prospect, especially for those close to me. I was warned about the possible hatred directed at me from both pro-choice and pro-life camps. My testimony was fated to be misunderstood.

The other choice would have been to just remain silent. Yet, the fact that my personal experience of pregnancy and abortion is a difficult thing to understand did not seem a good enough reason to dismiss it. Furthermore, that clandestine abortion is a thing of the past does not make legalized abortion a "normal" event. Those who choose to have one, no matter the reasons, tend to remain silent; a veil of secrecy hangs heavily. I, myself, have eluded until now my feelings about abortion and about the identity of an embryo and a fetus.

This testimony, though, does not grapple with the political issues revolving around abortion, nor does it have anything to do with illegal, unsafe abortion, a historical and important concern for generations of women. Instead, my story is an exploration of family trauma, self-inflicted wounds, compulsive patterns, and the moral clarity and moral confusion guiding my choice. This story won't fit neatly into the bumper sticker slogan "my body, my choice." In order to protect reproductive freedom, many of us pro-choice women usually choose to not talk publicly about experiences such as mine because we might compromise our right to choose. In opening up the conversation on abortion to the existential experience that it can represent to many, for the sake of greater honesty and a richer language of choice, we run risks.

Abortion is a painful event brought about by inadequate actions. "Pro-life" advocates exploit and sensationalize the experience and ignore the mistakes. One such human "mistake" is the economic pressure compounded by ignorance that is the most common reason for undergoing abortion. It is inevitable to see an anti-life sentiment in the pro-life movement when it protects ignorance by opposing family planning, sex education, and informed use of contraceptives. A recent article in the *New York Times* disclosed Latin America's abortion statistics and the alarming results of a rigid fundamentalism combined with poverty and ignorance. The United Nations reports that over four million abortions, most of them illegal, take place in Latin America annually, and up to five thousand women die each year from complications from the procedure. The rate of abortions in Latin America is forty per one thousand women of childbearing age, the highest outside Eastern Europe.

These figures reflect, among many things, the ineffectiveness of teaching abstinence as the only form of contraception, which is the general program followed by churches and schools. Latin America holds some of the world's most stringent abortion laws, yet it still has the world's highest rate of abortions. In the United States, however, where abortion is legal and sex education is broader, the abortion rate reached a twenty-four-year low in the 1990s with its lowest level in 2002, when there were 20.9 abortions per 1,000 women ages fifteen to forty-four, according to the Alan Guttmacher Institute. Nevertheless, Western European youths who are as sexually active as American girls but have a significantly greater exposure to sexual education and informed use of contraceptives, are seven times less likely to have an abortion and seventy times less likely to have gonorrhea. It becomes unsustainable to identify at any level with the "pro-life" movement when it fundamentally calls for the United States to regress to Latin America's horrific abortion and female-mortality figures and bluntly ignores Western Europe's impressive low abortion statistics.

As much as I am determined to tell the account of my addiction to abortion without dwelling on the political and philosophical debate surrounding *Roe v. Wade*, I cannot go on without acknowledging that thirty-three years after the U.S. Supreme Court delivered its landmark ruling, states are placing an increasing number of restrictions on abortion. The ruling gave women a constitutionally protected right to choose abortion in the early stages of pregnancy. Unlike "pro-life" beliefs, the ruling acknowledged and addressed the fact that the human missteps leading to the painful reality of abortion, like the psychological ones afflicting me or the economic ones pursuing so many, are beyond control. Thus, a nation's obligation to ensure a woman's right to life and health—which anti-abortion laws violate—had to be the overriding principle. With the alarming increase in abortion limitations, the missteps and lapses that make up the reality of abortion can only be compounded.

Mine is a story that in part reveals the lack and then emergence of a sense of responsibility when I exercised my right to abortion. I want to explore how when abortion takes on repetitive and self-mutilating qualities it can point to an addiction. In the process, I hope to address questions that might elucidate how pro-life and pro-choice advocates are, as it is with many profound and extreme human positions, both right and wrong.

For years, it didn't occur to me that there was anything to tell about abortion. Quite the opposite. There was much to forget. But I discovered that many other women were hungry to come to terms with a past scarred by cowardice and the need to cloak themselves in someone else's power. Many had a history of repeat abortions. They, like me, were eager to find a language to articulate an experience they had seldom spoken about. My testimony is not unique. Beyond the antiseptic, practical language of Planned Parenthood and the legalistic or moralistic discourse of *Roe v. Wade* and its pro-choice and pro-life counterparts, there are few words to articulate individual, intimate accounts. About half of American women having abortions in 2004 (of 1.5 million reported) had had a prior abortion. Close to 20 percent had had at least two previous abortions and 10 percent three or more. A considerable number of these repeat abortions occur among populations with high levels of contraceptive use.

· · ·

"I had twelve abortions in eleven years and they were the happiest years of my life." (Fifteen in fifteen years, when counting three others by another man.) I wrote those words years ago, before I came to understand the truth. I know I'm destined to be misunderstood, that many will see my nightmare as a story of abusing a right, of using abortion as a means of birth control. It isn't that. My nightmare is part of the awful secret, and the real story is shrouded in shame, colonialism, self-mutilation, and a family history that features a heroic grandmother, a suicidal mother, and two heroin-addicted brothers.

I know this account can't resolve the moral dilemma of my actions. Yet, I wanted to understand the spell a pregnant body exercised over me, my flawed desire to become someone, or something, else. The diaries I kept guided me. My promise to the reader is to deliver an account of my addiction, a steady flow of unhappiness, the X-ray of a delusion, and ultimately, the redeeming face of motherhood.

Halfway through working on this book I got pregnant for the sixteenth time. I don't think I would have been able to give birth without the call to accountability and self-reflection writing this story down demanded. My daughter became the coherence emerging from the shameful mass of thirty-five years.

Yes, I was an abortion addict and I do not wish for a scapegoat. Everything can be explained, justified, our last century tells us. Everything except for the burden of life interrupted that shall die with me.

The body is not a thing, it is a situation: it is our grasp on the world and our sketch of our project.

SIMONE DE BEAUVOIR, *The Second Sex*, 1949

My recollections of my mother begin and end with a dance. The first is the sight of green sugarcane fields surrounding our house and my mother's long, black hair flapping in the wind as she practices her dancing while holding onto a palm tree. The beaten poinciana tree to the left of my mother and the coconut-littered grass hint of Hurricane Catherine and the year 1973. I know the precise date of the last: February 28, 1977, at my brother's wedding. I was eight years old. The ballroom was filled with bodies pressed close together, dancing a bolero. I followed my mother's eyes to a corner of the room where my father's shoes moved rhythmically around red, high-heeled sandals. As they circled one another those four shoes barely broke their contact with the floor. My mother grabbed me by the arm and rushed outside, then smoked a cigarette by my father's car, talking to herself and occasionally kicking a tire with the heel of her shoe.

My father's final words to my mother were addressed to me: "Your mother doesn't know what she's doing." He was lifting her limp body off the road. I followed him closely to the car, with her bare lifeless foot clenched in my hand.

Shame runs back to the origins of my homeland. Staring at maps of Latin America, looking for my island, Puerto Rico is either absent or it appears as a territorial appendix. The maps dramatize the history of Puerto Rican dependency, first under Spain and then the United States. A testimony of selling out prevails; a people's willingness to barter national identity for economic gain has eaten away at our dignity and omnipotence.

My great-grandfather's dream of improving his life did not stand a chance when North American companies turned the island into a sugarcane monoculture. Lolita, his daughter, sold herself to the new owner of the coffee plantation he had worked for most of his life in exchange for rent. She was seventeen. My mother's birth was nothing but a remnant of a story of shame from time immemorial.

In the summer of 1940, two months after having my mother, Lolita boards a bus at the Plaza of Lares and sits down, squeezed between passengers and suitcases. She's a peasant from the highlands, a *jíbara*, and her face has that waxen pallor typical of country folks. She still has not shed the extra pounds she put on during the pregnancy, but all the same, she's a beautiful nineteen-year-old woman on her way out. If she didn't leave now, she would be trapped forever.

In San Juan, she embarks on a ship for New York, as many before and after her, to the land that pushed her out of her own to begin with. There she will come to see her compatriots as no better off in the land of opportunity than they had been back home and the forced migration of colonial peoples as just another form of subjugation. A life of servitude, just like the one she left behind, is all she will achieve.

Shame must have driven my grandmother away from Puerto Rico and walked by her side on the streets of the Bronx and in the sewing factories of the Lower East Side. It must have sparked her fervor for the leader of the Puerto Rican Nationalist movement, Don Pedro Albizu Campos, and sealed her martyrdom in 1954 as she stormed up the steps of the U.S. Capitol with a gun and a national flag in her purse. She served twenty-seven years for attempting to overthrow the government of the United States of America.

I suspect the history of my own shame and perhaps that of my mother begins with my grandmother's departure from the island. The first fourteen years of my mother's life were spent between different uncles' homes. She followed her grandmother as she shifted dwellings, first helping daughters-in-law with their new children and ultimately needing care herself when her tuberculosis worsened. When her grandmother was eventually bedridden in a hospice in San Juan, my mother remained with one of the uncles. I can only imagine my mother's shame through the secrets I have been told: men of Lares, some of her own blood, sneaking fumbling hands under her dress, thick fingers sliding up and down her thigh, and my mother watching the whole spectacle from a distance, as if she wasn't there. And then there is the one uncle she lived with when her grandmother left for the hospice, feeling her breasts, the one uncle she loves, cupping them in his hands, pretending fatherly affection. She smiles, laughs in that same knowing innocence, that feigned act that everyone who will come to know her would use to couch their advances. Even then there is no visible shame in her as she looks up at this one man and the others, for she knows already, with that instinctive knowing refined by years of being an orphan, how not to be in the way, amidst cousins who, unlike her, belonged to the home they were born in.

Between the uncle who violated her, the rich father she didn't know, the mother who had abandoned her, and the town that just watched, she was the gift arranged even before she knew it, the almost cliché casualty of colonialism. She was the sacrifice.

But she moved too fast for things to affect her. My father often described how he first saw her stepping out of a bus and walking down a hill, with that briskness of limb. She moved with a bold openness, careless and inviting, that narrowed men's eyes and softened women's hearts, and made everyone want to take her in their arms and protect her.

My mother married my father when she was barely fifteen, joining the Vilar household as a sixth child. My father's two sisters, not much younger than my mother, looked up to her. His mother, *abuela* Irene, quickly adopted the thin, undernourished girl as her own, while my father's father felt responsible for the daughter of a Puerto Rican heroine. Grandfather Jose Maria was a supporter of the nationalist leader Don Pedro Albizu Campos and once had cognac with him in the office above the church he headed.

The Vilar family soon learned of my mother's pleasure in making a show of servility. They marveled at her generous disposition and her ability to know what each of them needed before they themselves knew. Dishes were cleaned even if never used. When she ran out of chores, she would empty the cupboards in the kitchen and wash and polish everything she could find. This habit made the house cherish her and soon my father was chastised every time he said or did anything that would upset her or make her lose her appetite. My mother's web-like servitude, which trapped her as much as those she served, only grew stronger with the years.

I often watched my mother's ever-pleasing movements through the houses we were guests in, and the hosts' grateful, submissive welcome. To this day I can't stop myself from taking over people's kitchens and washing their plates.

The only photograph I have of my mother where I can clearly make out her eyes is of her sitting on a low cement divider, her hands clasped together on her lap. Two long braids come down her chest and curl at the crease between her breasts and her full-term pregnant belly. I am inside her.

There are eight years between this picture and her death.

That last night at my brother's wedding, I wanted to remind my mother that the woman in the red shoes was her own beloved cousin, Teresa. But you couldn't speak to my mother when she was talking to herself. This was one of the few moments she could forget how much she loved you. Most of the time she acted with such adoration that nothing else mattered more than what she could do to make you love her. I learned to accompany her silently during the times she seemed troubled and busied myself waiting for the dark cloud to pass. This time the cloud would stay put.

In the hour or so from the moment I knew my mother had died until my father arrived at my uncle's house, I locked myself in a bedroom where I kept running, bumping into furniture and trading hiding places. I closed myself in a closet and pulled every hanging garment over me until I was a pile of clothes. Under a bed I curled against the wall moaning and hid my face in the corner. Behind a desk I no longer cried but repeatedly bumped my head on the wood. At some point, I was afraid and had to leave the room to go looking for my aunt. When my father arrived he sat me on his lap and before he could open his mouth I told him I knew. Mom had left. Then I told him not to worry, that everything was going to be just fine. I knew how to cook rice and would do it every day, starting tomorrow. I was a stoic little girl comforting her father and telling her aunt she needed a black outfit for the funeral.

Everyone opted to believe that my mother had fallen out of the car while she was sleeping when the door suddenly opened. They must have suspected the truth, for they had basked in my mother's devotion and feared the consequences, the price she was bound to pay when she realized that no one on Earth could reciprocate. This suspicion and a feeling of complicity was probably what forced the silence and distance between my families.

• • •

The day she chose to jump out of our lives, my mother left behind an eight-year-old girl and a forty-year-old man fearful of questions. She also left my three brothers, Miguel, 15, Cheo, 19, and Fonso, 20. Only recently have I given any thought to what her death could have meant to them. As for me, no one in my family ever asked how I felt. No one ever spoke about what happened. The night of my mother's death my father and I drove to the hospital in silence and have remained silent on the subject to this day. We did sit in a room at the courthouse days after and were asked questions. We looked into each other's eyes trying to offer some comfort and that was that. Father was not after answers and that is what made up his charm. He brought this carefree aloofness to life when he took to the floor and danced his brains out. He won the dance floor time after time dancing cumbias and salsas and merengues, and he continued the dance in the kitchen, making us all eat away our fears. He went about his business humming, singing, or joking, and telling everybody who came to him with a trouble or two to eat a good meal or have a drink and then see how they felt. I remember him throughout my childhood, handing out a plate brimming with rice and beans or a shot of rum.

We never took the risk of asking questions. That was the police's job. Our job was to go on living without leaving any more corpses around.

For a year or so, we lived alone at home, my father, Miguel, Fonsito, and myself. Newly wed Cheo lived in San Juan with a wife who tended to his nineteen-year-old broken body. He couldn't walk after a car accident, a year before the wedding, left him paralyzed from the waist down, with a blown up bladder, urethra, and prostate. We visited Cheo every weekend on our way to see Grandmother Irene. Each time my father stopped at a bookie in the corner of the apartment complex and bet on horses for his son. In Cheo's tiny apartment, I played cards with my brother's wife while my father's big arms carried my brother to the tub and gave him a bath.

My mother's absence made little difference to the house, except that she herself was no longer in it. I often roamed the quiet rooms with a blinding, almost obsessive desire for constant action: sleepovers with cousins, hunting for seashells, best grades in the classroom, collecting comic books, memorizing Christmas carols, flamenco dancing, masturbating, anything that kept me from feeling a thing.

I busied myself fetching land crabs and memorizing songs I would sing to my father at bedtime. I sorted the laundry for him when he washed our clothes and held the bottle of starch while he ironed my school uniforms. I sat in the hallway and sobbed when he cleaned the diarrhea-soiled path from my bedroom to the bathroom, all the while telling me I was his baby girl and humming his favorite song about an old horse that can outrun his young. I had chronic diarrhea until I got my period at eleven. I remember because I sprang to the toilet after messing the bathroom floor at boarding school to find my underwear soiled red. I don't recall any more accidents after that.

I see my father in the kitchen of his small restaurant on the beach pounding an octopus. The restaurant was his pastime he practiced after work and on the weekends. I think the hangout was also his protection from the voracious, needy love of my mother. He often took me there on Saturdays and had me rinse the conch shells after he got the meat out. I would dip them in a water bucket and then scrub the hairy algae or tough barnacles off the shells. Each time I got to keep one and take it home. I despaired over which shell had the best sounding sea inside. They all sounded different and the same. Many times, at the brink of tears, I had Father choose for me.

In a way, I always felt safe with my father and in danger with my mother. Her love for me was as passionate and all giving as her love for my father, but it was expressed in waves, alternating with periods of unnerving silence and neglect. One night she protected me against a robber at the doorsteps of our house with her teeth and nails until the bleeding man ran away, and the next, she left me alone while she walked the cane fields at midnight or went looking for my father.

She could be odd and unpredictable. For my seventh birthday she committed to baking a cake for me to take to school. It was her idea. She told the teacher and I saw them chatting away about my cake. Getting into the car the morning of my birthday, I asked if the cake was in the trunk. She said there was no cake. I cried all the way to school. When we got there she opened the trunk and took out a giant three-layered chocolate cake with a little water fountain in the middle and a golden fish swimming inside. She took my face in her hands and asked: "How could you ever believe I didn't bake you the best cake in the whole wide world?"

Needless to say, I ran to the safety of my father's arms every day at five o'clock when he came home as if for dear life. And yet, all I wanted was my mother's happiness. When she died I should have felt like the most terrible person on the face of the earth. But I don't recall feeling anything like it.

My father introduced me to Blanquita as a good friend who wanted to throw his daughter a nice birthday. She moved in with us over Christmas, nine months after my mother's death. Immediately afterward, she set out to refurnish the whole house, especially my parents' bedroom. I recall following her every movement, in love with her, wishing for her attention, admiring her blond hair held in a perfect bun, and her tiny ears pressed against her delicate head. She spoke often of her three daughters whom she'd lost to their rich father in her divorce. She couldn't see them. I was jealous when she showed me their pictures. I remember that well. I wanted to be my stepmother's daughter and she reminded me with her faded pictures that I wasn't.

Since my mother's death, my brother Miguel had been spending many nights at schoolmates' homes in town. When he returned, he always had friends with him, so he never had time anymore to push me in the swing, climb up a tree, or listen to me sing. Once I found him sitting alone in the palm grove and asked if he would jump on the bed with me. He said Blanquita did not like him inside the main house. Another time he was locked out of his one-room studio, which was attached to the garage, and came into the house. I ran toward him, but before I could get there Blanquita asked him to wait out on the porch. She said he had muddy shoes. I saw him look at us, her arms wrapped around my shoulders, and I was ashamed.

Then he disappeared. I overheard Blanquita tell my father she hoped he would move out for good. She said he was taking drugs. My father said he would be back. He'd run away many times, though never for so long, and each time he'd stolen something from the house, from a relative or a friend. Blanquita said it was dangerous for me to be exposed to Miguel. Every day after school I would go into my brother's room and look at his things. I missed him. I would sit on the bathroom floor smelling the half-smoked joints and tiny roaches piled up in a Coca Cola crystal ashtray by the tub. I would sing the Christmas carols I'd memorized from a booklet he had given me. Between songs, I would stuff my mouth with toilet paper, a habit that would last until I left home for boarding school a few months short of my tenth birthday.

I begged my father to let me go live with Uncle Jose and Aunt Betsy. They were moving with my three cousins to a school in the snowy woods of New Hampshire where sweet deer napped right on the yard and let you pat them. My uncle was to teach Greek and Latin in exchange for free tuition, room, and board. The head of the school, Mr. Boynton, had been my uncle's and father's teacher at an Episcopalian private school in San Juan back in the early fifties.

The morning I left for the airport, we found Miguel sleeping on the floor of the garage. From the back seat of the car I saw him wake up to the sound of the engine. My father's head turned away from my brother as he backed out of the garage. Blanquita was worried about missing the plane. I rolled down the window and called my brother. Then my father stopped the car and got out. I saw him take money out of his back pocket and give some to my brother. Miguel stared at the bills in his hand. Then he looked up and saw me. He didn't look like my brother.

• • •

In the woods of New Hampshire, I turned to religion, wanting to be a saint, an elaborate guise for nostalgia, for my mother, my father, and my family. I roamed through the pastoral life with Bible in hand. The maple tree forests were home to a God against whom my mother's absence, in both life and death, and my father's aloofness were no more important than cutting a tree down for the school's wood stove.

Over the two years I was away in boarding school, I returned home four times. Nothing and everything had altered. My mother's sadness and laughter accompanied me as I took my unspoken questions from room to room. Sometimes I had an impulse to ask my father about the things that worried me. I watched him and waited for the right moment, which never came. He was like an important and loving stranger with no time to spare. And I, I had no words for my questions. I walked through the house when no one was around and stared into each room, newly decorated by Blanquita. Only a mural in my father's bedroom drawn by my brother Cheo, a rainbow arching over my parents' names, pointed the way back.

Miguel was away each of the times I went home, twice in rehab, and the other two times in jail for drug possession. On Sundays at my grandmother Irene's, the family would gather and recount all the things they had lost to my brother—VCRs, TVs, cameras, checkbooks, phones, books, a Salvat encyclopedia from one uncle, and a Britannica from the other one. Many objects from the churches my Episcopalian uncle headed had disappeared as well. Crosses, communion trays, silver altar candlesticks, band cinctures, a gold leaf baptismal round base, and pulpit stoles. My grandmother would change the subject, reprimanding her children over such talk, and explain that her grandchild was ill. I remember feeling proud that my brother only stole from family and friends and never from strangers.

The summer before I turned twelve, my oldest brother, Fonso, lost his job, his wife, and two children to his drug addiction. Everyone in the family was stunned. He was twenty-five and had a seemingly solid character. In July of 1981, two of my brothers were in jail for possession. And Uncle Jose and his family were moving to Baltimore and not going back to New Hampshire. I was stranded at home and seldom left my room. I dreaded Blanquita's hovering over me, frantic that my father no longer seemed to care for their relationship. She asked me to beg him to marry her. She told me of his other women. She knew he didn't care for them, though.

I wanted to run away, go back to Boynton School or live in San Juan with my other aunts and cousins. When my father's Spanish uncle and his family came to visit us in early August, I saw my way out. And so did Blanquita. She offered to take us on a vacation to Spain. Once there, I asked to stay. She enrolled me in a Catholic boarding school a few hours from my family's small town.

Twelve years old and lonely in a convent school for girls in Spain, I am sitting on the edge of my bed when I see a slim book on my roommate's night table. The cover shows a girl my age. I open it hoping for a romance novel. I read diary entry after diary entry expecting the story to take off, but what takes off is the sweet character herself along with her whole family to a place of no return. *The Diary of Anne Frank* left a mark, more like a scar, and I treated it by starting my own diary. It was the beginning of an infinite series of failed attempts at keeping a schedule that was not set by anyone else but me.

The scar I carried had little to do with the horror of the Holocaust, which I had no sense of, but rather it had to do with a girl who wakes up in an attic every morning and has to go about the servile duty of asking permission to exist in that smallest of holes. She does not have to ask this of Hitler, but from her peers in that attic. This was my life ever since my mother died. I became a damned guest child, waking up in different homes, among aunts, cousins, family friends, and lending a hand to my father's busy schedule. I had to beam a big smile at my generous hosts and ask permission to occupy some place in the world. I woke up each morning wondering what others thought or felt about me. Was I in their way? My incessant monologue, this ongoing translation of other people's feelings and actions, I saw in Anne Frank.

A year and a half later, I flew back to Puerto Rico for my father's wedding and moved in with the newlyweds. After close to four years in boarding schools in the United States and Spain, a placement exam made me a high school junior at thirteen. Myrna, my father's wife, was a senior and three months pregnant. He had met her at a cafeteria near her school and across the street from his office. She not only had my mother's name, but also her zodiac sign. The first days after the wedding, I sat on a stool at the kitchen counter and watched her cook. I didn't know if I missed Blanquita, but we had lost all contact and it didn't feel right. The few times I asked my father I was told he didn't know where she lived. He had heard she had moved in with another man. This fact felt as off as the three years separating me from my new stepmother. I followed her movements in the kitchen with mounting anger. She was shy and clumsy and did not know how to cook. I refused to eat her meals. One early morning I found her crying in the kitchen. My father had not come home. Soon enough I saw her tears give way to a sadness and neediness that was simply my mother's. I then turned toward her. As her pregnancy advanced and my father continued staying out late, she became angry.

When my sister Diana was born, in February 1983, my stepmother was the unhappiest woman I'd known. When Diana came home from the hospital, I held her all night. She was colicky and my stepmother's cesarean prevented her from pacing the room without doubling over in pain. Often, during that first year of her life, I would rescue my baby sister from her mother's sadness. A few times, I kept her away from my parents' fights. Dad, still up to his old tricks with other women, would come in late and my stepmother would cry. One day she lashed out at him and I caught the baby in midair. When she grew ferocious, possessed by jealousy and anger, she reminded me of my mother even more.

Fifteen months later, another daughter, Mirilde, was born. Myrna was eighteen years old and at a loss with two babies. Each morning I left for school I worried for them. When I came back I babysat while my stepmother finished her senior year in high school at night. At times, she seemed happy. When they were together, my father spoiled and cared for her. But just like with my mother, he could make her feel needed and important one minute, and then the next minute he would choose everything, dominoes, horse races, another woman, a baseball game, the newspaper, over her.

I grew closer to my brother Cheo, who now worked with our father. He had gone through multiple surgeries and could walk again without catheters attached to his thigh and waist. He picked me up from high school often and drove me home. He liked to distract me from my questions about Miguel and Fonso with stories of our mother that I was too young to remember. One day he was unusually quiet. He asked me to open the glove compartment and look at a pink slip of paper. When I could not make sense of it, he told me he had cancer of the bladder and that it had spread all over his body. I cried on his lap the rest of the way home.

As all of this was taking place around me, I discovered the heroism of my grandmother and made her my love object. When President Carter pardoned her in 1979 and she returned to Puerto Rico, I saw her often whenever I visited the island. Once I moved back from Spain for good, I spent many weekends at her apartment. I wished to become a revolutionary to "free" my island of colonialism, and study political science in college. Each time I saw her, she reminded me to address her by her name, "Lolita." When she spoke of my mother she called her "Tatita," never "my daughter" or "your mother."

Once, I asked her why.

"Tatita is her own person. She is not yours nor mine," she said, pointing both her index fingers up at the ceiling.

I saw my grandmother's blunt disregard for my feelings as sublime honesty. In part, perhaps, because I needed her to be just that: Lolita, the heroine.

The threat of loss became the air I breathed. The dramatic, deadly power struggles that propelled almost everyone around me, and in the case of my mother had resulted in tragedy, wedged me into a corner of exacerbated obedience and compliance and action. Today I know that I grew to experience any conflict, the fabric of growth, as a menace. During these crucial formative years no one significant in my life, except for my uncles and aunts on my father's side, modeled a power struggle that could end in a good way. I evaded all conflicts and did not stop moving, aiming to overachieve at everything. I was perceived as the most passionate, all-giving, and submissive little girl who had ever set foot in the world. I was my mother's daughter, even though I had the assurance of being my father's daughter. While Father came to me the way day and night come, predictable and constant, Mother had come to me the way falling stars come, by luck, by chance, by sheer magic. As present as she was, she could be equally absent. Her ever-shifting states of unhappiness and manic love always kept me on alert. Years later, while sailing back and forth across the Gulf Stream, I would feel her presence when I was at the helm during night watches. At first I believed those long hours of random thoughts were bound to evoke one's mother, but now I know better. She was there in that cockpit with me because I was there alone, on watch.

In time, I stopped feeling lonely. I turned my mother's absence into a benign anxiety, a longing for a life devoid of power struggle, and privately made for myself a world out of that hope and oblivion.

The summer night of 1984 I packed for college, my little sister Diana sat in my suitcase and would not get up. She cried and then squatted and peed on my clothes. She slept with her arms locked tightly around my neck. In the morning, she pulled my younger sister's crib to the floor with the sleeping baby inside. I flew away to New York feeling I was abandoning her.

I was fifteen, and relatives and family friends thought my father was setting me free too fast, too early. The days after he dropped me off in the college dorm and flew back to Puerto Rico, I was lonelier and more afraid than ever. I walked three miles every day to an English language tutor I did not understand. She served me perfect miniature triangles of deviled-ham sandwiches and iced tea. I listened to her talk about one son who died in Vietnam and another son who lived in Hawaii and never called. Her home was a dark dungeon of war memorabilia. Each day for a month, I walked to and from this woman's house and wished I could leave college and go home. I just wasn't sure where that was.

I visited the bookstore every day on my way from English tutoring. Amidst books I felt less lonely. One day I saw a shelf dedicated to books about adoption. One had a picture of a dark-skinned, Mexican-looking baby who stared at me with pleading eyes. Counting my last dollars, I quickly chose the books over food for the weekend. Often, during the first two semesters of college,

I blotted out my paralysis and anxiety, especially in bed at night, with fantasies of mothering the children in those books.

Alba was my first real and important friend at Syracuse University and in my life. We met in my sophomore year. I loved her from the moment Ivan, my Venezuelan boyfriend, introduced us at the student organization he ran and where Alba was the director of cultural relations. She kissed me twice, once on each cheek, and with a big smile asked where I was from. I couldn't take my eyes off her long, blond hair. It ran down her shoulders, parted at her breasts, and kept going to her waist where, depending on her moves, it fondled her hips. She was a big girl, dressed like a hippie with no makeup, and yet she could as well have stepped out of *Vogue*. Her eyes were smart and pressing for every answer, while her smile didn't seem to care.

I told her I loved her hair. She told me she loved the country I came from. I said I wished I had a country. "You know, Puerto Rico is a colony, truly," I told her. The notebook she had been writing in when I came into the office, the notebook Ivan called Alba's official log of human miseries, led me to think she would approve of such words. She was in the habit of writing down trivialities she deemed worth remembering. She also drew in that notebook. There were faces of people and things that came her way. They too seemed to hold meaning she wished to save. Needless to say, I wished to be in her notebook.

Somehow she, too, loved me and showed it by inviting me to her house. Her father, a poet and professor of Spanish literature on campus, knew of my grandmother Lolita and had even written a poem in her name. Mercedes, her mother, was cold and distant. She went on about how dreadful America was and Syracuse in particular. She seemed bitter and wasted by the smoke of the constantly lighted cigarettes on the coffee table. Nevertheless, the subdued anger she felt toward her husband for having taken her away from Spain and the life she could have led, found its way into a dark humor that made me laugh so hard I was ashamed. There was no increased tenderness from Mercedes when she found out that we both had lost our mothers at age eight, but unlike with her daughter and husband, I was never the subject of her pointed jokes.

I was in Puerto Rico over the Christmas break of 1986 missing Ivan when the phone rang with news of Alba's car accident. Mercedes could barely speak. Alba was alive but her friend riding in the passenger seat was dead. Alba hadn't eaten or spoken a word in two days. I promised I would be there in no time.

When I arrived at their house and opened the door to Alba's bedroom, I could smell the pain. She lay in bed staring at the wall. Her blouse was stained with blood and so were parts of her hair. I held her in my arms until my strength gave way. First, she just hung there, then she began to sob quietly, almost without emotion, until the sobs gave way to trembling. Then, almost magically, she fell asleep and a faint, melodious snoring filled the room. At that point, I could dare to picture her in the car turned upside down, trapped awake and alive under the body of the Chinese friend. Death had lain on her for close to two hours.

We walked in silence every day for hours. I forced food into her with the threat of my own hunger strike. I warned her that I was a hundred pounds, and I would hit ninety and inevitable anorexia by the start of classes, if she didn't eat. I would probably need to take a leave of absence. I bathed her and slept with her and locked her feet between my legs, just in case. She slept in an almost horrifyingly deep sleep until one day she woke up with a smile and told me the twin bed was too small for the two of us. I felt I had given birth to something beautiful.

Mercedes started joining us on our walks. Slowly we made it into town, went to old vintage stores, walked farther out, explored neighborhoods, and bought things we didn't need at garage sales. Back in Alba's room we exchanged clothes and read aloud to each other until one of us fell asleep. Our friendship grew into this ceremony and never did moments of indifference, misunderstandings, or doubts enter in.

"I·wish you were a man," I said to her in my mind many times.

"I wish you were," I would have her answer back.

Outwardly, I hugged and kissed and pulled people along. Sadness did not exist. Inwardly, I wasn't sure what I felt or where I was headed. Loving and caring for Alba gave me some direction. Outwardly, Alba was in a state of chaos and confusion. She couldn't see into this chaos beyond the philosophy books she was reading on the death of God and meaning. It sucked her into caves of blind suffering. She thrived in my need for action, found refuge in my compulsion to keep on moving, in the little girl in denial who ran my life by dodging all conflict and achieving at all costs. But no matter her own brand of fears, inwardly Alba's nature was order, clarity, purity. She looked upon emotions like anger, jealousy, and despair with the knowledge that they could be dominated, and she refused to be devastated by them. Having agnostic Mercedes as a mother must have helped her develop this shell of confidence in reason, but she also had Spain's quixotic, hardheaded history to thank. I could sense that country through the clothes that filled her dresser; they traced her entire life.

Even the house held things from generations back, books, paintings, furniture, a collection of earrings Alba had pinned to a piece of embroidery of her grandmother's. I couldn't recall having anything more than a few years old. I watched Alba brush her hair and felt that there, too, in the extraordinary length of it, lay the constant time and history I didn't have.

By the time Ivan arrived on campus at the end of January 1987, I was someone else. We went to the movies and I couldn't stop thinking of Alba. Was she okay? Was she at home or walking the streets alone like some frenetic gothic character? He would caress my breast or slide his hand down my trousers and I would see her lying in bed, staring at the ceiling. I began to choose her over him.

One evening I refused to sleep with him because I had to go to Alba's house. He suggested she was a lesbian. I said he was crazy. Soon after that exchange, my roommate told me she had seen him kissing a girl in my car. I said it was impossible; the man had principles. He would never do it in my car. So I began to visit him at awkward hours. One night he sent me away because he was too busy to take a break. He asked me to call before visiting. Back in my dorm I called a friend from class and invited him for dinner. It wasn't a week before Ivan knocked at my door and found out one meaning of visiting people unannounced. We finally broke up after having been together for two years. As for me, it was April and I was about to flunk the semester. But it wasn't that bad. I had Alba.

The month of May arrived and found me in quiet disarray, stuck on campus with an incomplete grade. My anthropology professor suggested I go to Mexico City and do research in exchange for credits. I would continue what I had done for him during the semester, count dead people from seventeenth-century colonial church registers and input their race, age, the cause of death, and so on into spreadsheets. When he and his colleague published their book on infanticide in Mexico during colonial times, they would acknowledge my research. Alba said she would come along. I didn't need Ivan after all. Traveling alone with my best friend seemed almost worth the price of separation. We flew down to Mexico

the day after classes ended and moved into a hostel for the summer. I couldn't have foreseen then that this trip would lead me to
hit bottom before losing all belief in myself.

It all seems to begin and end in a house that filled me with
wonder and an unprecedented longing. The anthropology professor's old mansion stood in the historic center of the Zona Rosa
in Mexico City. The walls were cracked and the floor had caved
in. Out in the courtyard, by a small fountain, was an old bench. I
sat on it. Under my feet a pattern of delicate pink flowers faded in
and out from tile to tile. There was a special beauty to the thin
grass growing between them. The breeze gathered inside the walls
of the patio and played with my skirt. A very sweet and pungent
smell of gardenias clung to the air I breathed.

I had never encountered such particular decay mixed with
beauty. I came from an island. I grew up with little knowledge
of history. It was hard to attach something as big as history to an
island. Perhaps that's why it had been easy to leave in the first place.
My experience of time was of weather and oblivion more than of
history. We had hurricane seasons making sure that what man
failed to ravage, nature did. We had our own decrepit version of
history. We didn't have significant civilizations waiting for Co-
lumbus, elaborate calendars to refer to in the future, silver or gold
or expanses of land to sustain an oligarchic class.

I had been born in the New World, on an island that spoke
Spanish, the language of the Old World. The Spanish language is
filled with history and I think this is what I sensed in Mexico and
in Alba, in this crumbling courtyard and in that home of hers. My
tongue, the Spanish language, had a home but my body did not.
My body remained part of a fragile landscape with no passport of
its own, stuck within a hesitant country, an island adrift between
Old World empires to the east and their independent colonies to
the west, and between the new empire to the north that I lived in

and the nationalist grandmother to the south I couldn't stop thinking of.

In a way, this rift lay at the heart of my having shamed my way
through Mexico. I did it with such ferocity and with such despair
that it was almost as if I envied the crumbling courtyard that I had
seen at the old mansion.

First was Rodolfo. He worked in the same wing at the archives. He
counted his registers of defunct people with utmost concentration.
I ignored him, confident that sooner or later he would rise from the
dead. He did. We had lunch at his mother's house and the following Sunday he took me to his best friend's wedding. I have no recollection of that day except that I lost the heel of my right shoe and
limped my way back to the hotel room humiliated. The feeling increased when he just said goodbye at the door and left. The next
day at the archives he greeted me by lifting me off the floor. He smiled
and basked in his powers. Well, look at this guy, I said to him in my
mind, I'll give you something to bask in. That evening I did.

"From looking at you, you'd never tell what a woman you are,"
he said.

I ran my hand down his back in appreciation. He smoked,
propped up on the pillow while I, my knees drawn to my smallish
breasts, wondered why this nice man wanted me. He caught my eyes.

"What are you thinking with that busy brain?"

Suddenly his smile reminded me of Ivan's smile, a smile of
narcissism and mischief. No woman I knew smiled like that. I
began to avoid him.

I then met Timothy during breakfast in the hostel's cafeteria.
We discussed Joyce and Ireland's civil war. Before I knew it, I was
upstairs on his bed looking at the pen samples he was trying to
market in Mexico.

"Do you mind this?"

He took his jacket off, dropped it on a chair and moved toward me. I saw how milk-white his long neck looked in his open shirt and when he reached for my waist it didn't feel right. I couldn't stop thinking about his neck and slim, lengthy body as he caressed me and we undressed each other. It was awkward and cold and unfamiliar until he picked up my body and sat it on top of him. When I felt him inside, stiff and big, taking hold of me, my thoughts and doubts were brushed aside. He seemed familiar. But the moment he came out of me and caught my eyes, he was an awfully white, slim boy from faraway Ireland and I was lost again.

I met the Aztec at a phone booth a block away from my hotel. It was midday and I needed to call a bank to check if my father's money had arrived. I had been broke and hungry for a couple of days now. The woman I spoke to told me it was Friday and there was nothing to do until Monday. I hung up disheartened. A voice behind me, very close to my ear, asked me if I needed a ride some-where. I turned and saw a tall man with a very Indian face, but propped too high for a Mexican. His manners were unusual. After an introduction, he asked me if I wanted to have lunch with him. He knew a wonderful Japanese place nearby. I had never eaten Japanese food before, but I was hungry. On the walk there I no-ticed a calm about him, which made the city, and myself, seem noisier. He breathed deeply, noticeably, and I asked him about it.

"Yoga," he said.

He did yoga even when he walked. At the restaurant I said I had no appetite. I had no money to pay and was ashamed to eat if he paid the bill.

Back in his nice apartment by the telephone booth, he showed me his library and asked if I wished to play chess. We played one game that I lost within minutes. He went to the kitchen for a drink.

I looked around, hoping he would offer me a snack, and noticed there were teddy bears everywhere. Fearing he might have some dangerous fetish, I was looking for an exit when he came back and explained that he had a daughter from a previous marriage. She came over every weekend and each time he waited with a new teddy bear.

He moved upon me and I wondered whether he could have any idea that I was hungry. I promised myself I would eat afterward. I would not be too shy to eat from his kitchen, no sir. As I became driven by this resolution, he was already inside me, I held on to this stranger out of sheer hope he would touch my soul, understand it for what I didn't so that I wasn't alone.

I knew I was losing my bearings. I did it regardless, opening my eyes, which I always kept closed, seeing only his cheek, closing them again, moving back into my numbing darkness.

This ritual repeated itself for a day and a half, while I was literally a missing person. At some point he lay on me and said:

"I'm sort of getting this need for you, aren't I?"

When he dozed off, I got out of the bed and stretched out on the cool floor. On the white wall opposite me were some framed photographs: pyramids, ancient masks, an empty plaza, a picture of a Buddhist monk. I thought about this odd man linked to me, this apartment filled with teddy bears, the white walls with his pictures, and the cars whisking by below.

I had to strain to remember Alba streets away, my college life in Syracuse, my own father. I put on my clothes and ran for dear life. On the way out I stole a loaf of bread.

The summer of 1987, when I went hungry in Mexico, was the preamble of the story to come. Today, I can safely say that my

mother's death confirmed and made redundantly real the impotent feeling every child fears and works so hard to vanquish. A
natural narcissist at heart and a programmed resilient survivor, I
worked hard at achieving importance. I obsessively worked to
banish the terror of my smallness. In the end, the ways I solved
my yearnings for meaning and importance became the story of my
life, the choices I made and the lies I told.

To overcome anxiety and make the world a safe place, a reality we
control that serves us, transference becomes a passion to be healed
through fulfillment in another. For Jung, transference is a necessary projection to bear life, oneself, and the disillusion that comes
of knowing that we are ultimately alone to decay and die. Ever since
I can remember, but especially since the night of my mother's
suicide when I clung to the physician's white coat and would not
let go, I have wanted to forget my impotence and chase away all
anxiety at all cost. A blinding longing for control shaped my days.

Goethe wrote in *Wilhelm Meister's Apprenticeship*: "There are
no means of safety against superior qualities of another person but
to love him." I understand Goethe. For close to a decade I followed
one man's ideas. He seemed the most powerful, the one in most
control. I patterned my ideals after him. It is as simple and vulgar
as that. My first book was a memoir that today reads to me as proof
of the lie I have at times made of my life. I told a clear-cut story
of three generations of woman in one family (my grandmother,
mother, and myself) intent on self-destruction against the backdrop of political struggle. The transference horror script I lived
out with the man I loved and became pregnant by multiple times,
as I wrote my life down during those years, is absent in that memoir, tucked away under the noble rug of family history. The story
I told was true, but it could have been truer.

Writing down this other story, here, I've discovered that my personal history alters constantly as more is "remembered" or released into my consciousness, recasting in this way my sense of self and the lives I've led. There is a frightening continuity and discontinuity when I think of my past and my present. How different I have been. But even more frightening is the awareness of how entirely other I might yet become.

In writing, a heightened awareness seizes me, and I realize a truth is buried somewhere and it's all up to me, and the words. Right now, I must make my way through what appears to be an insoluble problem. Though my delusions have been a result of being hopelessly absorbed with myself, of seeing in life only what I need to see, I'm choosing the method of memoir writing, which is in itself self-absorbing. At seventeen, just as when I was eleven, and before that a child, a toddler, and an infant, I was absorbed with myself. I still am.

Erich Fromm wrote that man's natural "narcissism" is inevitable; it seems to come from our animal nature. Through ages of evolution we've had to protect our integrity, preserve our physiochemical identity. In man, physiochemical identity and the sense of power and agency have become conscious, so that narcissism is inseparable from self-esteem. But the thing is, because we are a product of a world of symbols, our sense of worth is constructed symbolically, on ideas of our own worth. We build our selves up at the same time we grow more certain of our impotence in the face of death. It's a hopeless fate. Are we to blame for lying to ourselves?

In a way, one could look back at one's life and grasp its meaning by asking how conscious we are of what we do to earn our feeling of worth. In my case, I see an underlying terror of admitting that I was hiding in the cloak of someone else's power.

A willing, proud servant was how I saw myself until very recently. Albert Camus wrote in *The Fall*, "Ah, mon cher, for anyone who is alone, without God and without master, the weight of days is dreadful. Hence one must choose a master, God being out of style."

Here then, meet my master.

He was a professor of Latin American Literature and Theory, which gave him the official outlet for his gifts as lecturer and thinker on the go. There were stories about overcrowded classes where students showed up unregistered even though the class was filled to capacity, and about audiences standing for hours way back in the hallways, cheering the professor's genius turns of thought, and still other stories about student body protests in front of NYU's chancellor's building demanding the renewal of a teaching contract for their fashionable professor when there was a rumor he might be let go.

His other pursuit was writing, and apart from a mild degree of fame that had come from his years editing a journal and publishing his friends Julio Cortázar, Carlos Fuentes, Gabriel García Márquez, Manuel Puig, and Octavio Paz, the journal brought him nothing, but also took nothing out of him. He had been writing a novel titled *Agatha* since the year I was born. Aside from the occasional luminary essay in his own journal, he had not published at all, not from any mistrust of his own power but from sheer inertia and something else that eluded him. He had too clear a perception of the significance of his talents ever to doubt himself. He seemed to act or not act according to some belief that his genius thrived inside a ticking clock with an alarm set to awaken that genius at special times.

He was an Argentinean philosopher, and a Jew by ancestry who had studied in India before the Beatles discovered it. He was the survivor of a student generation decimated by a dictatorship's secret police. He was a protégé of the Ford Foundation's man of letters, Kalman Silver. He was the product of morning's national schools and afternoon's yeshivas and evening's tango dungeons—things that the mother of his first wife, Camilla, would call an abomination, but good Catholic Camilla called a prophecy. Both twenty-one, they had met in a class on Buddhist philosophy and decided to marry by semester's end. The aristocratic mother-in-law came to his small apartment overlooking the port of Buenos Aires and threatened to have him arrested if he didn't leave Camilla. She said: "I will never allow my daughter to marry a communist, a philosopher, a bum, a Jew."

He asked: "In that order, ma'am?"

The marriage lasted only six months.

I can't help seeing his life, as I know it, as a story of my own desires. I picture him as a sixteen-year-old running back and forth between a yeshiva and a public high school, in the midst of Peronist times, and in his mind, sketched like the city he knew by heart, the thirty-two secret paths to wisdom. Our studious young man knows each of these paths is responsible for the whole of creation, and what is more, he can give examples during his Talmud class that make the rabbi look out the window in exasperation.

As he leaves the yeshiva and heads for the soccer field, the city shaking with the hope night brings, he draws a step sideways and one backwards as if tracing his own footsteps all the while humming a tango he'll practice with the new household help. Much later, when everyone has gone to sleep, he'll go to her room and once again feel his hand burn against her sex and then feel all that desire pulling him in to the extent of his hope, the place where all thirty-two secret paths to wisdom meet. He looks up. About him he sees Rome and understands why all roads must lead to Buenos Aires.

At twenty-six, ten years later, all roads led him to India. He had been close to finishing his degree in Philosophy of History when the panic attacks came back. His friend the psychoanalyst advised him not to worry, a trip to India would take care of it. He suffered for months before his departure, a pain so piercing he was certain he would die.

He told me once that the attacks had begun with the disillusion he experienced when he found his sister cheating on her husband. Four years his senior, she had introduced him to everything that had turned him into the man he was. Heifetz, Freud, Marx, Walter Benjamin . . . But then when she was sixteen, as if she had glimpsed her face in the mirror and in horror saw into the great woman she could become, she agreed to marry the son of Rabbi Polanski, an aspiring rabbi himself. They married a year later and with that Rebecca Polanski turned her back on the city that raised her and her life potential. Not for long, though. She bore a son and soon after began a series of affairs with her brother's friends that caused her demise. She fled to New York.

His panic attacks returned when a scholarship was offered to him to conduct graduate studies in India. His psychoanalyst friend encouraged the change. It all happened too fast. One morning he stood in the dean's office being granted the scholarship, the next he lay on the couch at his friend's office, and the following day he was taken to none other than the president of the republic. Here, at la Casa Rosada, the leader of the nation signed the government edict subsidizing the cost of his studies and the journey via ship. He had requested an ocean journey because the crash that killed the tango singer Carlos Gardel had made him incapable of setting foot on an airplane.

The morning of his departure, hundreds of his students and friends from Buenos Aires University came to bid him farewell. It was 1961. The ship sounded its horn, yet there was still no sign of his father. His mother had hugged him goodbye but not his father. At the last moment, when he was climbing up the gangway, his ex-wife Camilla shouted out to him that the father was there. He turned and saw him, standing under a tree, wearing a black suit and hat as if dressed for a funeral.

His father, Noe, had served his family. He'd served his wife, his daughter Rebecca, but particularly he'd served his son. Where he had been curtailed in life, his son would fly. It must have been his dream. But for his son, that freedom foreshadowed a break with his father, and this premonition hung over his shoulders. Both destinies, his father's and his, were scrambled together in his imagination. Every time he read a line in a book that impressed him with its wisdom, he would think, if only his father could read this and understand.

He refused to take over the silk factory his father had worked so hard to establish in a new country, all for them. His refusal, shortly after abandoning the yeshiva, to study philosophy at the university, coupled with the news that he was marrying a non-Jew, were blows to the father. He grew increasingly silent but accepted his son's wishes. When his father did speak, he used that uneasy mixture of Yiddish and Spanish that felt like a burden to his son.

It was India that finally broke their relationship. His father told him, "You are sailing off to India to study a religion that has nothing to do with anything. Son, I don't like it and I don't understand it."

Something tells me that it was this day, his nose pressed against the invisible wall that rose between his father and him, that he acquired the poise that baffled people and intimidated me. He had a way of greeting that seemed more like a farewell, an air of always being on his way.

India turned out to be just like it sounded, feminine and too big and a little cruel. The first week he arrived, he was sitting on the terrace of the Banares apartment he had been given overlooking the Ganges. A smell of home hit him and made him hungry. He looked around but there was no sign of grilled meat. Moments later, walking the river banks and watching the beautiful Indian women lifting up their saris as they dipped their bare legs, thighs, and arms in the sacred river, he understood the smell for what it was. Behind him a thin and wrinkled man carried a cot over his head. The man walked with difficulty under the cot, which was soon revealed to be carrying the body of a woman, painfully beautiful and asleep. They both went down the steps that led to the water and stood in line for the boat that was to burn the dead. The hunger that had struck him quickly changed into sheer shock and shook the ground he stood on.

A year later, he circled the whole continent by jeep. He met the Mexican writer Octavio Paz, ambassador to India, and they struck a friendship that changed his life forever. He returned to Banares convinced he didn't want to be a professional philosopher, if there was such a thing. He wanted to be a writer. He left India for Italy, and on the boat he met Emma, the Australian woman who would become his second wife.

After working as a teaching assistant in Rome, he returned to Buenos Aires, where he was given the chair of the late university professor who had sent him to India in the first place. He only lasted a day on the job. His new tenure coincided with the military takeover of the university and the firing of a whole generation of thinkers. They tried to force him to stay under the precept that the government had paid for his trip and studies in India, but he could not comply. His long pilgrimage began then. Over the next decade, most of his childhood and college friends who remained behind would disappear at the hands of the military secret police. His last visit to Buenos Aires was in 1981 to arrange his parents' safe passage to New York.

In America he founded a literary journal and made good friends. He housed the writer Borges, his former teacher, for weeks at a time. He wore long, purple velvet pants to class and despised both his Wasp and Anti-defamation League colleagues. He taught the French theorists before they were translated into English. He separated from Emma the Australian and moved on to Kathy the Jewish aspiring Broadway actress. Finally he met Ada, the Argentine ballerina turned psychology student. We met after he split from her.

He would tell you that his life story was one of a break with the past, but a necessary break. I saw something of value in this fracture, something that worked for me. His break with the past, which he wore on his sleeve, became a haven for me.

I was sixteen and he was fifty. I was tired and he was healthy. He was a professor and I was his student during that fall semester in 1986 before Alba's accident. In class I saw him leaning on the chalk holder of the blackboard, one hand carelessly hanging by his side, the other holding a blue pencil he stared at while he told us the story of quitting smoking:

"It happened," he says, "that in my life I loved many women, and many women loved me. I also left many women, and yes, many women left me. Friends, well, they came and went, and so did I, but one, only one was there all along by my side, loyal like no one or nothing else, ever. He was my constant other, that's what he was, some mirror of God perhaps, and here I was deserting him, my faithful, beloved Marlboro cigarette."

He laid the pencil to rest and turned his eyes to us. What can I say? He was beauty, beauty chiseled out of words, wrought in flesh, marvelously graceful.

"You see," he continued, "dark things are not so that we may be filled with horror, nor are clear things so that we may sleep in peace. Basically we always recast stories to suit us. The trick then is to turn ourselves into truthful events so that it's not all in vain."

Then he showed us the game of the bird's view, his way with stories, of getting at what you could not otherwise get at. I tried it myself. I closed my eyes and for the first time in my life, took a bird's eye view of my early youth. It was not that far away. I could see certain rituals, some initiations. Going up and down trees for example, and swings and rooftops, wandering about things, peeping out at them, and hiding the double life I led since my parents split it with their drama and then my mother with her death. When I opened my eyes, there were his, on mine. Maybe because I had flown a little too long, but there they were, a perception of such weight and density that left me speechless and longing for that one word that would make us, me and the truth in his words, one and the same.

I went to see him in his office right after class. First, I stopped in the bathroom and examined myself in the mirror. I unbuttoned my blouse enough so my cleavage that still had not developed could pass for a chest he might rest his head on. He was sitting behind his desk, his hands brought together as if in prayer. He signaled me to sit down and while running his eyes over me and resting them on my neck, asked me what I had meant by the word *substructure* in my essay on García Márquez's *One Hundred Years of Solitude*. I said, stupidly, I'd learned about structure in a book. He stared at a spot behind me, lost in thought, while embarrassment rushed to my face and a cold sweat began to collect on the palms of my hands. He walked toward me, stood behind my chair looking for something on the bookshelf, and just as I closed my eyes to draw in his body closer to mine, the heat given off by his waist burning my neck, he handed me a book. The title read *Justine*. I looked up and he said:

"Lawrence Durrell is the author for you.

"You are a seducer," he went on as he walked back to his desk, "you must know that, Ms. Vilar, do you? *Justine* will do you good."

He had astonishing beauty, infallible charm, and an accent in both Spanish and English that made me vibrate. When he spoke my name with that South American cadence, it felt like a caress. It was the most unhurried voice I had ever heard. It said the oddest things, too, and took the longest pauses, as if each of his words deserved the respect of thought and so you, too, felt respected. It was the opposite of the silence I got from other adults when the absence of words felt more like control.

I could scarcely look at him. In his face you could see that many of the hues and curves of youth had carried over to manhood. There remained in his deep-layered wrinkles, especially around the mouth, relics of a boy. Or maybe it was just the influence of the picture I had seen in his office. Taken in the late thirties, a boy sits on the groomed lawn of a park in Buenos Aires, a big bow tied around his neck and the placid hand of his mother on his tiny shoulders. The boy is staring with big, intense eyes. He stares at the cameraman and not the camera. There is a hint of mockery in those eyes as if the picture was being taken the other way around.

This way of looking remained with him, so that a pair of intense eyes, hazel green, set deep below long lashes, took you in every time they met yours. His hair grew on its own accord; there was no sign of a comb having run through it or a hairline. He knew he was a disturbingly handsome man. He walked unassumingly, and with a faintly perceptible bend, different from a bowing of the shoulders, more like the posture of a soccer player about to kick.

His irreverence shocked me. Nothing withstood the heavy load of his intellect: family, education, books, love, God. Nothing was sacred to him but the ability to smell the rat. In less than an hour I learned that families were nests of suffering, education a farce, books an absurd attempt at eternity, love a recent invention, God a dream gone sour. I went back to my dorm after the office visit drenched in desire for this impenetrable, impossible man, and for freedom from the pettiness of feelings that weighed down on me. My roommate, a graduate student, had taken his class a few years back and told me to beware. "He's dangerous," she warned me. "Everything that comes out of his mouth touches his students. He's merciless."

She accused him of trying to turn people's lives upside down for the sake of teaching the value of freedom. She told me that one day a student complained about the reading list, saying she didn't find any relation between the list and the subject of the class. He said Marquis de Sade was mandatory reading if she was to understand anything about literature. If she didn't see that, she could do him the great favor of dropping the class. The more terrible my roommate painted him, the more of a wolf he became, and the more I wished I could be a lamb.

Afterward, alone in bed, I reenacted every single gesture of his, thinking that in spite of the tenderness in his smile one could not fall for this man immediately. There was that hard, straight thing about him that in itself gave an impression of excellence, forcing you to step back, never forward. But this was at the beginning, before that other thing about him was revealed: his complete lack of the rotten smell of a liar, the malodorous substance that I noticed many times rising from my own body. This is why, perhaps, when the time came the following year, I was the one to make the first move.

• • •

He found me walking on campus early one October night in 1987 and offered me a ride home. On the way, he pointed at the moon.

"A good moon for sailing," he said. "A damn good moon to look at from the water."

"Let's look at it," I said.

"But the water," he lamented.

"Hey," I encouraged him, "isn't this Finger Lakes country?"

We drove for an hour in the midst of a snowstorm until we reached the shores of Skaneateles Lake. When he offered me a bite of his roast beef sandwich, I said no thanks. I was too hungry. There, as I watched him breathe in the evening air, hands in his pockets, eyes turned inward, I came to feel rammed against something grand, and so I kissed him. I would have died happy just then, for nothing had required so much of me ever before or since. When later that evening I bent over a car seat for him and became pregnant for the first time, I felt nauseous with hunger and told myself I had to handle my finances better, save money for groceries instead of wasting it all on presents for friends. Each month, as his business suffered, my father's allowance for room and board arrived increasingly late. He was unable to shower me with the steady and exaggerated flow of funds that had marked my high school years and in part cushioned our crippled relationship, and I proved ignorant and reckless in managing money. I took Alba to dinner and then had no means to buy food for the rest of the week.

As the new day rose behind the car, I told him about me. He listened. I could see he was slowly falling for my fears. After some silence, he kissed me on the forehead and said that one never remembers the past clearly and dispassionately. Each of my memories, like our dreams, stand for something else, that was all.

It wasn't long, maybe a week, before he said something like this: *I have this liking for you and it is for your sake that I feel we must agree to behave with prudence and not let us be seen together.*

His words sounded so cautious that it was hard to believe he was aloof and disinterested in me. Had he been able to speak more frankly he would have probably said something of this sort: *I like you very much but it is impossible that I should ever consider you more than a plaything. I have greater priorities in my life, my writing and my freedom.*

Over Thanksgiving break he invited me to visit his sailboat with him. Looking out from the deck of the boat over the calm harbor of Greenport, NY, with the glow of sunset still on it under a starry winter sky, I felt hopeless in my smallness. But then a man in the boat yard below yelled up to us, "That's one fine lady of a Swan forty-four. It should be rounding off Cape Horn instead of jacked up on dry land." Amused by the compliment of the fellow sailor, he turned to me and said he wondered if this was a sign of the life we could have.

"We'll have to see if you have what it takes," he added, tapping the anchor windlass with the back of his shoe. "It takes a lot to take on the horizon, you know."

I murmured, "Thank you," and looked away.

Our relationship had to be hidden from the world, for my sake, but not on the boat. On *Sarabande* I could prove I had what it took to make my presence in his life worthwhile. In all, I felt flattered at seeing him assume a responsibility that was not really his, warding off danger from me. It made the affection he offered me seem tender; such was the poverty of my character.

The important duties that preoccupied him did not include me. They were his parents, recently flown in from Buenos Aires, who were old and feeble and alone in a God-forsaken city. Who could live on a two-dollar-a-month government pension? And there was

Rebecca, his sister, one day here, one day gone, living half of the year in Yucatan, Mexico. In the pictures taped to a small blackboard in his office she was tall, with big black eyes and an expressive face glowing with mischief as she tickled a Mayan boy. She was several years older than he but younger in character. She seemed loving and unselfish and had carved her way in life, the first to leave Buenos Aires and set foot in New York in the 1960s. He called her another casualty of his homeland. His contempt for the country he loved so much was another matter of greater importance than I.

He spoke as if his life had been weighed down by the burden of these lives bound to his and he acted as if this weight of responsibility obliged him to move cautiously through life and set his freedom above love and the like. At the age of fifty-one, the desire for love had not yet escaped his heart but it seemed pinned down by a sense of bitterness and frustration at the thought of all the delays it had caused him in the past. About him there was this mistrust of himself and of the past weaknesses of his character, which he coined "the romantic in me."

Then, there was the sailboat. I would say the sailing, but of this there was and would be little. What drove his passion was the resolve to never attach his life to a house. He called a house a coffin and often made the point that homes stifled his imagination and turned it into a meander of useless thoughts on the past. In homes he wrote like a romantic, whereas on a sailboat he wrote like a mercenary, intent on a mission above and beyond people and their antics. Indeed, it seemed to me that what he would come to write during the seven months we lived on a sailboat in the Bahamas each year was philosophy more than fiction.

He lived in a perpetual state of impatient expectation of something that was to evolve from him through his brain, basically art, and of something that was to come to him from outside—the right lifestyle, enough time on his sailboat, commuting to New York City (Syracuse was a threat to the condition of his gray matter).

He loved to move, to travel, and to dip his feet in seawater. He loved to stare at the horizon and repeat Pascal's words: *perdida, perdida por buscarte* (lost, lost for having searched for you). He loved Montauk's white beaches, flashing lighthouses, glossy breakers, and horseshoe crabs fleeing sideways, which he called a crabby tango. He loved to lie down and warm his belly on the hot sand. Above all, he loved to do this in the company of a woman. Except something troubled him about this: he might have to pay for the company with his freedom.

I first read Paul Tillich when I was pregnant for the first time. I have a clear recollection of reading *The Courage to Be*. The professor had put the book on reserve at the library and I sat there reading all afternoon into part of the evening. There was a limit of two hours on the book and I had to keep renewing it, fearful that someone else might come to use it and that the librarian might grow restless with me, and somewhat ashamed that I didn't have the money to buy my own copy. So I hid behind a bookshelf in the back of the room, stressed out, and on the lookout.

Tillich's New Being touched me deeply. His New Being had to have the "courage to be" himself, to stand on his own feet, to face the contradictions of the real world. The task ahead for every human being was a sort of cosmic heroism. I had to have the courage to face my anxiety of meaninglessness and to recognize the ways I sheltered myself in the powers of others.

"I can be a mother, can't I?" I thought, feeling urged on by Tillich, uplifted, filled with hope. His words made me think about those years in boarding school when I wanted to be a saint and roamed the woods of the New Hampshire countryside, certain of God's existence and my own goodness. Those times, when I was eleven and believed I could do anything, remain the most centered moments of my life. Six years later I was a doubtful, shaky teenager. Reading Tillich, I glimpsed the cocoon I was building for myself, the bug life I could not see but suspected in my guilt-ridden days when anything I did felt like a contraption, a utilitarian action to ward off loneliness. Sexuality spun a casing of shame around me, slowly concealing my origins and ties to my past. But pregnant, my life felt less sub-human. In this unique state I felt hope.

Alba took me to her mother's gynecologist for what she said would be a quick fix. That's what she called it, a quick fix, and the abortion was so quick indeed that I did not have time to be afraid or even cry. Only months later, in the parking lot of the rundown medical building in downtown Syracuse where I'd had the abortion, I let out a tear. It ran down my cheek, one thin tear; while the other half of my face remained frozen and dry. I had not thought of birth control. My only thought that night I had sex with him in a car was of making sure I was not in the way of a man's pleasure and my running.

After the abortion, I left Alba as soon as I could, assuring her I needed to rest. But instead of going to my dorm, I limped my way to the School of Arts & Sciences, hoping he would be there during his office hours. The moment he saw me, he asked why I looked so pale and I hinted I had my period.

Later that day, at his apartment, he lifted my body and sat it on the counter by the sink. He said a woman's days were the safest to make love. While he proceeded to find his way inside me, I closed my eyes, tightened my lips, and swore I would kill myself if I let him in on my pain. I kept on hearing him speak in the back of my mind. The words hushed the pain. They told me how women's desire for children killed each one of his love stories, how each of his companions couldn't endure the high price it takes to live a life in freedom, how his relationships never lasted more than five years, how hard he'd fought to remain fatherless and not be swept away by the fears of others.

The words turned in a circle and inside them I felt safe. It was like a lullaby of reason and measure, a cadence of idealism in the midst of my frantic, disorganized movement. Afterward, when his real voice commented on my period's incredible amount of blood, I remembered the doctor's warning about the dangers of repeat pregnancy following an abortion.

The next morning, I moved out from the two-bedroom, south campus apartment I shared with a graduate student and into a second floor, three-bedroom apartment off campus. I orchestrated the whole move to give us the privacy he needed. I sold most of my books back to the bookstore and begged my father for extra money to cover the rent and security deposit. He did not understand why I needed to live alone. I blamed it all on my roommate and promised I would find new roommates for the spring semester to share the rent with. I was physically and emotionally exhausted and yet I could not make myself stop. The landlord greeted me at the top of the stairs just as I knelt down on the icy path to the house from the jabbing pain in my lower abdomen. In one hand he had a bag of snow salt and in the other a baby girl.

I did little else but wait for him to call and come round. I would go to classes, do my laundry, read books, all the while daydreaming about him. Anything that interrupted my obsessive thoughts brought me back to a desperate and frantic state. I was not alive when he wasn't with me.

The only actions that summoned my full attention and desire were all related to him: reading about his country, his Judaic tradition, the Hindu Gods he was fond of, dressing up for him, arranging the apartment to his liking, buying foods he might enjoy, imagining our lives together on a boat crossing some tranquil ocean.

I had no future other than the telephone call signaling his arrival or my meeting him somewhere. I would try to leave the apartment as little as possible, fearing that he might call during my absence. Every time the phone rang, I was consumed with hope.

The days I did not see him I obsessed over what might have happened to stop him from seeing me. I feared his ex-wife. He spoke often of her and praised her. At twenty-eight, she was a talented ballerina, the daughter of an aristocratic Argentinean family, and a PhD student of psychology on campus. She had bought their sailboat with cash and supported his writing and lifestyle. When she became interested in becoming a mother and pursuing her studies, he told me, he packed up his suitcase and split.

One night when he was supposed to come by, he called to say he was meeting his ex-wife for dinner at a restaurant because she needed his advice. Of course, no problem, I said, and hung up in a daze, assaulted by the realization that this man I loved was a complete stranger. What did I really know of his life after all? As I always did when I didn't know what to do, I got into the bathtub. I took a hand mirror in with me. I studied my face and understood what he might think about me. I didn't amount to much. Compared to his ex-wife, I was nothing. I imagined him drinking his coffee, talking, laughing with his students, comforting his ex-wife, and thinking of their intimacy, as if I didn't exist. His indifference was crushing. Would he be astonished to find out that I never stopped thinking about him from morning to night? No, he probably knew, I thought, and the humiliation was comforting, almost reassuring, as it lit the flame of a death wish.

In the mirror, I swore I saw my mother staring back at me with a smile. I basked in the thought of killing myself, in the same way I would make love without birth control: without thinking about the consequences. That night was the first time I drank myself to sleep. The next morning I roamed the apartment unsure of what to do next. Go to class? I didn't want to miss his phone call. Go to his office? I didn't want to be a pest. Call Alba? She didn't approve of the relationship so when I was with her, I stopped myself from speaking of him and that was a bore. I sat at the kitchen table and stared at the mess in my apartment and the moving boxes still needing to be unpacked and waited for the phone to ring.

Leaning against one of the boxes was my mother's picture blown up to poster size and in a metallic frame. It was my brother's idea. The enlargement blurred her eyes and made the mole on the right corner of her chin a sort of accident, something that didn't belong and prompted you to look away. I did and saw his book on the chair opened to the page he'd last read. The pen I'd given him was there, in between the pages. It was a gold leaf fountain pen that had cost me three hundred dollars, close to one month's allowance for groceries and spending money. The pen was the reason I was so broke and hungry. Each time he took me out to dinner or lunch, I was terrified. He expected me to pay for half of everything; he said it was the only way to escape a father-daughter objectification of our relationship. At each restaurant I told him I wasn't hungry or that I had just eaten and then watched him eat away wondering when I would have the courage to order a meal.

When I think of our first year together my stomach tightens. Such was the hunger I felt. Weighing 105 pounds at five foot six, pictures of me show a skeletal figure.

The phone finally rang. He asked me to join him and a colleague for lunch on campus. I said I would be there in a minute. He was introducing me into his world. When I hung up I realized I had no money to pay for lunch, nor the rent for that matter. The eviction notice was by the phone. I went back to the kitchen table and sat there, exhausted. His ex-wife probably treated him to their dinner the night before. She still lived in what had been their home. Once in a while when he couldn't find something of his in my apartment, he would say, "It's probably at my house." What I heard was, "Ada is taking care of it." My poverty would surely remind him of the woman I was not yet, the burden I might be. I began to cry, tears of defeat and resignation. My mother's picture stared at me, and this time I didn't look away. In a little over a month, I would attempt suicide.

I went home over the Christmas holiday in 1987 because that's what I was supposed to do each Christmas. He was back in New York, living his life without me. At night, when I went to bed, I closed my eyes and saw his trademark red scarf wrapped around the neck of his ex-wife and his hand on her delicate ballerina shoulder. In the nightmarish fantasy they were always standing under the arch of Washington Square Park in the Village watching mimes' funny moves and laughing. I opened my eyes and stared at the old ceiling fan dangerously spinning too close to the bed, wanting to blot them off my mind. On each of my arms lay my sisters' heads, four-year-old Diana and two-and-a-half-year-old Miri. The feel of their small bodies cut me like an indefinite pain.

In the day I was restless. I wanted to play with my sisters, laugh, chase the chickens up the hill behind the house, catch lizards, take showers together, but instead I was anxious around them. Their neediness, which once had prompted me to love them even more, now repelled me. When there were any disagreements between them or between us my heart pounded hard and I was out of breath. Any conflict made me easily angry and stern. When they cried, I stared at their tears with an eerie coldness that scared me. I felt defaced. When they looked into my eyes I felt they knew what was wrong. I wanted to run away. I invented reasons to be out of the house. The girls went with their grandmother while Myrna worked part time at a store wrapping Christmas presents. Once I was alone, I missed them and felt ashamed of escaping.

At home, I could not sit still long enough to watch a soap opera, which once, not that far back, had rooted me to a couch for evenings in a row. My father had found as much pleasure in coming back from work and seeing me fixed to the TV screen as he did when I read books. No matter that people said a thirteen-year-old should not watch so many soap operas or read so many books, he thought that in me they would be fertile ground. But this time I could not stand the TV nor could I pick out a book. I was making my father anxious. He avoided looking me in the eyes. I sensed he felt there were many questions behind them. What was worse, I wanted to clean up my mother's grave.

Driving to the cemetery, I told myself I would never neglect my mother's grave again. Seven years had passed since my last visit. I was an eleven-year-old industrious girl then, propelled by a pastoral, utopian life in the woods of New Hampshire. But now, walking between graves, I grew restless. I lost my way. When the undertaker pointed at a frayed Puerto Rican flag hanging from a pole not far from where we stood and looked admiringly at me for being Lolita's granddaughter, I was short with him. What was with the tall grass anyway? It was hot in the midday sun and there was no wind. I returned to the car bored with the whole idea. I left the unused bucket and rags in the parking lot. On the drive back home I looked out the window at the landscape of my childhood. It was ugly, alien, and disturbingly familiar.

Early in the morning of New Year's Eve Day I stormed into my father's bedroom and asked if I could leave. There was a flight just before noon I could make. Nothing he said could change my mind: "Your uncles and cousins are expecting you in San Juan this evening."

"Your grandmothers haven't seen you since last Christmas." "Didn't you want to visit your brother Miguel in jail?" "What about your little sisters? Only the other day you cried on the phone over missing them." Finally, he said, "I won't pay for the difference in the ticket." When he asked what was wrong, I answered, "This man, Papa, the teacher I told you about, he's waiting for me and I love him." He shook his head and threw the newspaper on the floor. "You are crazy, child, but go, go if that is what you want." He paid for the ticket and sent me away with an uncharacteristic severe look in his face. Only past the security check, when I turned one last time to wave good-bye, he smiled. It was a smile of regret and relief, and I wondered if he was feeling the same thing I had felt with my sisters.

At Kennedy airport, I saw this teacher of mine walking toward me, hands in his pockets, and I was confident, cheerful, clairvoyant. I had fallen under a spell and shut down my guards, not that I ever had many.

My first time in Manhattan, New York seemed a city of women and pretzels. The party at his friend Ursula's did not start until ten that evening and we went to a dimly lit café where you could sit in easy chairs by the fire. The tables were inscribed with signatures and sayings. I read them looking for the obscenities I was used to seeing in public bathrooms at home but these were beautiful and sounded like poetry. The waitresses, in miniskirts and black stockings, moved quickly around us, and they were heavily made up with Cleopatra eyes. The bartender was a woman too. Her hair was on fire and she ate maraschino cherries one after another. She had waved at him when we came in and I think she also winked.

"Nancy!" he called to a pleasant-looking woman wearing shorts and high boots.

"Mito!" she screamed back, walking to our table with arms wide open, kissing him straight on the mouth.

Nancy was charming and straightforward and shook my hand without rancor. When she spoke she looked at me often as if she'd known me as long as she'd known him. She had a little sparkling diamond in her left nostril and later she said she had another in her clitoris. They talked about the good old times.

"Remember that night on Spring Street?" she asked, and he shook his head and laughed.

"You know," she said turning to me, "this man was the best-looking man in the whole city. He wore these beautiful purple, velvet pants to class and the lines to hear his lectures went way down the hall and down the stairs. You see, there was no book that could give you what the sight and the sound of him gave you."

He shifted in his chair with some discomfort.

"Come on, Nancy, if I'm so great, why don't women give me tenure? I never get past six years."

"Ah, but that is because you haven't found your soul mate," she answered, and placed both of her hands on his knee. "Maybe she's sitting next to you as we speak." She looked at me with deeply set gray eyes that were now serious and frank. I loved this woman.

He pinched the back of her neck tenderly.

When she said good-bye she asked him to not get lost this time around and to beware of the Hamptons. Summers on his sailboat and too many evenings with William De Kooning were keeping him from the real world of the big apple.

"Why did she call you Mito?" I asked after she left.

"That's the nickname they gave me back in the old days. Mito, you know, as in Myth. I still don't know if it was because of the classes I taught or the clothes I wore."

"And who's De Kooning?" I asked shyly.

"A great painter who is now old with Alzheimer's. We used to spend a lot of time together but this last summer he mistook me for his father. It was difficult to have a conversation after that."

On our way to the party, I summoned the courage to ask if Nancy had been his lover. Yes, she had. But more that that, she had been a good friend. The previous spring, after he had split with Ada, he told me, Nancy arrived at his studio in Tudor City, the one we were staying in, and without saying much proceeded to give him the best sex of his life.

"She's great," he said. "Her only problem is that she's perfect already. She was from the beginning, you know, and that kind of perfection makes people stay put. They think they don't need anything. I can't travel with women like that."

"Are you saying that you couldn't love her?" I asked him.

"I'm saying, Irenita, that I need an unformed woman, unfinished, with not too many wounds. That's why I like young women. You, for example. But it's not only the age, believe me. I couldn't be with a young woman just for that. I would be bored to death. Nancy was young once and I could have had her if I wanted, but she was already old at heart by then. A woman attracts me when she doesn't carry a load of wounds that make her speak with such assurance and bitterness that I want to grab a *New York Times* and cut her off from my field of vision. Unfortunately, the laws of life are such that wounds pile up with the years. It takes a greatness of soul to escape this fate. Wounds are age. The more wounds you've got, the older and stiffer you grow. And you know, if you are stiff you can't travel, can't move. But you, you are young."

It seemed many women had a story woven around him. That they suffered or not with him wasn't as important as having become a better person just by knowing him. If you had loved him, you came back to the world a different creature, one that you might not completely recognize in the mirror, but liked a little better. All his ex-wives had gone on to build lives and have the children he refused to give them. They all still called him up on the phone. He said that they called to steal energy from him, some of the fire they themselves squelched by betting on the perils of domesticity and motherhood.

Emma, the Australian, golden heron dreamer of bush utopias, Kathy the Upper West Side New Yorker born to vaudeville, Ada the Argentinean ballerina he said "was crippled" by a career in psychoanalysis, and the first of them all, Camilla, the echo of his generation split between genocide, Paris, and New York like someone out of a Julio Cortázar novel. His women mesmerized me. I disliked every boyfriend I had had, every single one of them, because I was embarrassed by my old selves.

Ursula's loft was on Spring Street, the top floor of a tenement with an oversized skylight in the bathroom and a tub with too many feet. It was an odd place for such a skylight. You sat there on a gold leaf–painted toilet and tried to pee while looking up at the hole in the ceiling. The floor, radiator, and all the visible pipes were coated with golden dust, the walls were painted damask blue and a happy yellow I had never seen. The walls had been willed into art, so you walked in and it seemed the world walked about you. A life-size papier-mâché sculpture of Don Quixote on a horse stood by a large antique mirror with an ornate gilt frame. Together they greeted you at the door, Don Quixote and his reflection.

A gigantic reproduction of Velásquez's *Las Meninas* was painted on the floor and spread out across the entire loft. In the kitchen you walked over the dog from the original painting, only Ursula's was bright pink. Next to the bed, where we threw our coats, one of the servants looked out from under the bed frame. But unlike Velázquez's, this servant was black. The little girl princess of the painting was nowhere to be found and when I asked Ursula she said, "La princesa c'est moi." For the first time since my childhood days fetching sea crabs in the sand, it was fun to look at the ground.

Up above it was not as much fun. People wore black and looked at me as though I was a child awake past bedtime. I wished I had put on mascara and had worn a different outfit. As it was, I was wearing overalls.

I sat next to the kitchen entrance, by the pink dog, watching Ursula in a purple dress that followed the natural contours of her body like a second skin. She moved about constantly, throwing her long blond hair back away from her face, gliding forward to greet the visitors, and turning her face toward the center of the room where people mostly stood or danced. It seemed as if she set the whole party in motion. Juan looked at her while he shook his martini. Eduardo looked at her over his address book. The musician played for her, watching her over the black wings of the piano.

He came by and leaning against the wall, following my eyes, said:

"You can count on one hand the men in this room she has not slept with." He seemed bored.

"Narcissism in a man is not that attractive," he was looking at me now, "but in a woman it is catastrophic. It can waste away your youth and ill prepare you for old age. Look at her, in her early thirties, and all is gone."

I looked carefully for what she had lost. I could only hear her name being called time after time. "Ursula" they called, not because they needed to know where the bathroom was or the bar or anything about Ursula's life, but because she knew who she was, and therefore might also know, if only in bed, who they were. It felt like we were at sea and Ursula was our compass. She might have slept with every man in that room, but she had not stranded herself in their lives. Why else would they all still be fluttering around her, trying to assert their existence: I am a poet, I am a director, I am married, I have two children, I have built a house in East Hampton, I am having an exhibition, I published a book, I won a Pulitzer, I just returned from the Himalayas, I was promoted to executive editor, Art Forum is doing my piece, I am racing my Swan to Bermuda, I am Dean of Arts and Science. But none of these facts had the full-bodied power Ursula possessed when she said, "I am a painter."

Her beauty made me sad. I wished I could be her friend. I found my way to her kitchen and washed her dishes. She came by once and winked at me. I was grateful. Later she danced a tango with him while everyone stood by and watched in amazement.

At one point, she came by and sat with us. She wore opal earrings, bracelets, and a woody perfume. I could not take my eyes away from her neck. She used her hands like puppets, each finger with its role to play. She was joyful and seemed weightless, while her eyes scanned the room. She talked fast. A touching, apologetic smile accompanied her incoherence. She herself did not get lost in her speech, but she seemed concerned that we could not follow.

He wanted to leave. I could see it in his expression. He, who never swerved in the path of a drunkard or a beggar or potential robber, was bored with this beautiful woman. More than anything, I was discovering that he feared boredom, he feared women who snapped his interest in himself.

"I kind of like her," I said when she brought us drinks.

"You shouldn't drink," he said. "And good girls should be in bed early and not wasting their time amidst a bunch of drunks," he added, pinching the tip of my nose.

"I know."

He took the glass from my hands and emptied it into his.

"Then, that's enough drink for you."

Before I had time to protest, he started walking to the door. I caught up with him and wondered what I had done wrong. He put his arm around my shoulders. It was cold outside. He slipped his hand under my sweater. He squeezed my nipple, softly.

"You have great tiny breasts."

"Thanks," I said.

We walked in silence until we reached the train station. The streets swarmed with happy faces. In only a day, I'd met all these people who were chic and flamboyant and a pleasure to look at, and they spoke about themselves with such ease. If only I could learn the demeanor of an easy chair.

At the apartment in Tudor City, he looked at me for a moment and asked, "Do you want to sleep?"

I did.

"Not really," I said.

"Good."

His voice, his tone both of pleasure and surprise, sounded very far away. His tongue was hot and tasted of scotch. I tried to let myself go and threw my head back but he didn't let me. He told me to open my eyes. He turned toward me and placed his left leg between my legs. I felt my sex swelling as if it were closing of its own accord, just from the swelling, and it was doing so with something other than pleasure, what seemed an annoying, unbearable sensation. He asked me to take off my sweater and then slid the overalls' straps down my arms. He took a few steps back and stared at my white blouse. It was an old high school shirt I had worn under my blue uniform. He asked me to unbutton it. I had never felt as awkward struggling with the tiny buttons. The last one fell on his shoe just as his voice struck me with another command.

"Don't take off your bra."

"I always knew you were one of us," he spoke, slowly. "I've thought about you but I'd never thought you would be mine."

I wanted to run to the bathroom and fix myself up. I didn't like my smell or the sticky feeling in my hands. I felt suddenly angry. I could feel the tears swelling up in my eyes.

"I'm sorry," I said.

"What is it that I have to excuse you for, exactly?"

He knew perfectly well that his superior, formal, fuck-off tone caused women to tell him he had no real feeling for them and used this reproach to finally leave. Close friends had told him dozens of times to be more sensitive if he wanted to get beyond the six-year limit. If not, they warned, he would end up alone and die in bed without a love story cushioning the bare bones of death.

Now, this evening of my first tears, he probably glimpsed the eminence of secrets, stories, a bad script coming years in advance before the inevitable end of the relationship. But his grim voice and exasperated tone told me his heart gleamed a little. He passed a hand through my hair. There was so much of it and it fell onto my forehead all the time. I never felt neat, light, spritely, like Nancy or Ursula.

"I'm not pretty and I don't know much," I said staring at my feet.

He brushed my cheek.

"A silly girl you are!"

He touched my hair again.

"It would be good for you to put those two ideas out of your mind," he said. "You are my *alma gemela*. You are my soul mate . . ."

He grabbed me by the neck, tenderly, and pressed a hard, painful kiss on my mouth. He took me onto the floor, my sharp shoulder blades flat on the wood. He's lying on me, I thought. He desires me. I didn't want him to stop this time. Hands, buttons, zippers, all quicker than thought, feeling him move, knuckles scraping against my belly, my butt, oh please, please, why is it so difficult, why should it all feel like the end?

After, I don't move. I wait. And then I begin to cry, quietly, and I hate myself for it. I close my eyes. In the darkness I hear him breathe.

"What am I going to do with you? What am I going to do?" he murmurs.

He preferred to say little at these awkward moments, before the sadness that I could feel thriving under his armor of wit caught up with him. Why was he such a romantic? This he asked himself aloud at times. Women had made him lose precious time.

Time was running out and this little woman lying on the floor by his side, shedding some convoluted tears that most likely stemmed back to her own mother's womb—like they did with all his previous women—was going to require some heavy-duty work. Educating Rita. How many more women would he need to educate before he wrote his long overdue novel?

He got up. I heard him make his way to the bathroom. The light filtered under the door and I saw the line where my pubic hair gave way to the person. He came back and mentioned something about Freud and the unconscious.

"Tell me, Irene, what is the truth of those tears?"

It would take me more than a decade to understand the burden of such a question. Had he asked me simply, "What is bothering you?" I could have said, Nancy having sex right here on this fucking floor where I have no other choice but to love you.

Those were my simple tears. For him, they were the imminence of a psychological tic, a family history, my biography.

"One day you will write," he said. Only a book, he believed, could give truthful and transparent answers.

"Hear me right, Irene, Mallarmé knew it, the destiny of the world is to become a book."

On New Year's Day, he took me for my first real walk in New York City. From 33rd and First, we worked our way to Madison Avenue up into the sixties and back toward The Plaza on Fifth. He would never hold my hand. This was one of my early lessons. Holding hands kills desire, he said to me when I, timidly, passing my shopping bag to him, reached for his hand, and held it in mine. I quickly let go and thought that this one piece of advice, like not showering together or not brushing our teeth in front of each other, might be some genius secret knowledge one had to learn, for the sake of a future.

Men and women walked up and down the streets and the day seemed as though it could repeat itself for eternity. Even the people I saw in the streets after the party, huddled around trash-can fires or packed together sleeping under a tarp, seemed to be part of this grand design. I felt like an outsider, the single mortal, and what is worse, without a decent wardrobe.

He walked with his hands in his pockets humming a tango and I wondered how Buenos Aires was, if there, too, people seemed to live on air and the weird buzzing that fills the night. What did they live on back home, my home? As far as I knew, home was slowly becoming part of the wrong wardrobe, another index of things going cockeyed on me. I felt the weight of my origins when I sensed the reality of this other life in the north the most, when dusk fell before I had eaten my dinner or after I had gone to bed, and when I went outside after eating and the cold air stung my face, and a light breeze sailed through the treetops from which golden leaves fell in a shower. Nothing back home but fruit fell from a tree.

We went into Macy's. In the mirror by the fitting rooms he was trying on a new red scarf. He looked striking, the straight nose a radiant line from lower forehead over full, closed lips. The sight of myself in my corduroy overalls pushed aside all the excitement at being by this man's side. A couple of years earlier, overalls had been part of a utopian landscape of tapping trees and milking cows that I had mastered. In them, I had roamed the woods of a New Hampshire boarding school, certain of my goodness. They did not dress up a body, for I did not have one then. Overalls and work, movement, pride, and control all went together. Now, they stood for the exact opposite. And they exposed a body I wished I could blot out of my sight. I felt clumsy and awkward in comparison with him and his world, where everyone was confident and knew just what to do. I hoped I could shed my coarseness, my inadequacy, but I would never be like him or Ursula. I didn't have what it took, his aura of confidence, something intangible, an admiring audience, the profile of an exile for real reasons. Everything about him seemed to have been ordained from the beginning. I, on the other hand, felt like a scrapbook.

Back outside the clouds opened before a piercing sun. The windows glittered and I looked into them and wished for the day I could try on clothes in shops like these and dress like a lady.

Driving back to Syracuse, I told him about most of my life. Not that he asked. At the tollbooth on the George Washington Bridge, he had asked a question and the man answered in Spanish. When the toll collector said he was from Puerto Rico, I jumped in—"Me too, how nice." He looked at my excitement as if at a foreigner. Then, I did not understand the history of half my people who had migrated to this big city and made it their own. Bernstein's *West*

Side Story had given me a hint but no more. Nuyoricans were at home; this was their bridge, in a way, not mine.

As we drove away, he asked if it had been difficult to get away from my family on New Year's Eve. I heard myself saying no, it hadn't been a problem at all. I had a father that understood everything.

"Amazing how your father let you come to college so young. At fifteen you were almost a Lolita, one foot in the crib, the other in a man's bed."

I leaned back in my seat thinking of the Nabokov I had recently read in class and the movie he and I had once watched.

"Well, I haven't told you, but my grandmother's name is Lolita."

That's how the story of my life began, that day at least, as we drove up Route 17. Because he just knew, I'm sure, what this teenager by his side eventually needed to do to keep busy through his mornings of writing and his afternoons of reading; she just had to write her life story down during the day and meet with him at night.

But neither of us suspected the dilemma that would emerge when I—as author—made myself the subject of my own understanding.

L ater in January after our first New Year's together, doctors at the Jewish home in Williamsburg, where his parents lived, telephoned to say his father was close to dying. I begged him to let me go with him. He refused. Death is not a good thing for relationships, he said rather sarcastically, and his father, well, that was a touchy subject. He didn't want to share that with me, not now. I was like young Rostof in *War and Peace*. "Oh, to die, to die for Him! To die for the Czar. . . ." I felt a wounding desire to show my love in some way. He saw it, maybe, and agreed I could go the following day after I was done with my classes, but meeting his father or mother was out of the question. I saw him rush out of my apartment in the middle of the night with a somber look on his face and heard words to the effect of the time comes to each of us. He gave me a stronger hug than usual.

Back in bed I realized I had no money to pay for the bus. I put on one of his tango cassettes and served myself a shot of his vodka. I took it all at once and felt it mingle with my loneliness as I pictured him driving down 81 South to meet up with his father's death. I felt the need for something to happen, to fill the sudden awful space. I was pregnant again and the thought of it soothed me one minute and terrified me the next. I picked up the phone and rang my best friend, Alba. She was out. I headed for the bathroom and swallowed the entire contents of a bottle of extra-strength

Tylenol. I went to bed and damned myself for having spent my last dollars on that useless fountain pen. He had thanked me with a nervous smile—he didn't like gifts—and left it by the coffeepot. Now I couldn't take the 6:00 AM bus to show him how much I cared.

The doorbell rang and I woke up, startled. There was vomit all over me and on the floor by the bed. I opened the door thinking it was Alba. But Michael, my religion class's teaching assistant from Holland, stood at the door instead. We'd met in the library a few times and he had praised my comments in class. When he invited me out to dinner the week before, I said that would be lovely. I didn't care for him but I never said no.

"I'm sorry to storm in on you like this," he said calmly. "I was riding my bike and saw your lights on."

"Don't worry," I told him, "I'm actually in need of company."

"That's what I hoped." He spoke with the same serious and cold tone he did in class. "Can I bring my bike up or should I leave it out here?"

His direct, almost forceful words ticked me off.

"I don't care," I said, turning my back and heading upstairs. "You just brought me back from the dead."

Inside the apartment, he went straight for the paper towels in the kitchen and cleaned the floor around the bed. From the bathroom I watched him take off the sheets and search the apartment for new ones. He came to the bathroom and proceeded to take my clothes off. He did this mechanically and without asking any questions. He filled the bathtub, placed me there, and went to the kitchen where I heard him eating something. He came back when I was through and carried me to bed. I stared at this stranger's milky-white body as he undressed without a word. I couldn't string a thought together without meanings coiling into a hole. I closed my eyes and let myself fall in. I felt the heat of his body as he slid under the covers. I wished he wasn't in my bed. He fucked me with stiff patience for some time. I don't believe we said another word to each other that night or ever again.

In the late afternoon he called from New York City asking why I had made him wait at Port Authority like a fool. I said I missed the bus and I was taking the next one. He asked me why I missed the bus. I said I was late to the station. I was a wreck of lies.

How could I explain I had no money? How could I say I needed to wait until I found Alba to borrow it for the fare?

He had been thinking about me, he said with a more serene voice. He was somewhat worried because he had put together my clumsy gestures, my bumping into things all the time, my turning black and blue at these frequent accidents, with my constant breaking of glasses and now my missing the bus, and he had concluded I harbored suicidal tendencies. He actually called them self-destructive habits intent on becoming suicidal. He was quickly learning that my personal biography was fertile ground for multiple cautionary tales. His care and desire for me seemed to grow at their expense.

I asked how his father was doing. He had died in the morning.

Late in the afternoon, after finding Alba and borrowing the bus fare, I left for New York. The five-hour ride took forever. I realized I didn't know much about him. There was not much history to us beyond three or four months of lovemaking in hiding. But we had welcomed a new year together, I was pregnant with his child for the second time, and now his father had died. We were heading for some history all right. I only wished I had more to give him, money, presents, smarts, a family with a big old house, a country as rich as his Argentina, a prettier body like the ones of his beautiful ex-wives.

He greeted me with a smile and a tender hug. We walked in silence for a while until I summoned the courage to ask him about his father.

"He died of heartbreak," he answered, "heartbreak at seeing my mother lose her mind and get undressed in public every time."

His father had stopped speaking a year or so earlier. The doctors said it was senility but the son had told them it was depression. They all met, father, son, and doctors to decide what to do. He asked the doctors to listen as he asked his father, "Dad, do you want to live?"

His father nodded and that was it. His son insisted they treat his depression but no pill helped. The old man developed a cold that became pneumonia twice, and within a year of his wife's senility, he rapidly faded before everyone's eyes.

When his father died, he was looking at a catalogue of coffins with a man from the Hasidic synagogue that managed the home. He chose the cheapest, simplest coffin. His nephew was sitting with the grandfather. He told him his father went peacefully. His father had sat down on the bed, coughed once, and said the first words he had said in almost a year: "I'm cold." Then he lay back and died.

His hand trembled as he wrapped his scarf around his neck but there were no tears in his eyes. We got to his car and drove to Williamsburg where he had some business regarding his mother's care. As we entered the neighborhood, I saw men walking the streets like specters, with their black hats, long black coats, black beards, and ear locks. They were Hasidic Jews, some from southern Poland, some from Hungary. They had their own rabbi, a dynastic ruler who could trace his family's lineage back to the Ba'al Shem Tov, the eighteenth-century founder of Hasidism, whom they regarded as a God-invested personality, a prophet of sorts. I sat in the car peering out at this other world. The sun was low over the brownstones, all set tightly together like the men themselves hurrying in the cold evening. There were only minutes of sunlight left. Shielded between two men and a woman, a child walked playing with his ear lock, twirling it around his index finger. His mother tapped him on his tiny shoulder and he put his hands in his pockets. He looked up and stared at me.

At the nursing home, he refused to let me go with him. I begged and he turned away with a heavy sigh.

"Go on, then, go on and see for yourself." He sounded bitter and tired.

Expecting a terribly old and sick woman, I prepared for the worst. The home was clean and pleasant and filled with an infinite number of accents and languages. Healthy-looking men and women walked the hallways or sat together at tables in the reception room. I thought they were visitors as well but they greeted us and he in turn asked how the place was treating them. There were older, ill-stricken people, too, roaming the halls, but somehow everybody's eyes were those of youth. It was an anachronism of the flesh, I told him, and he smiled, softened now.

His mother had those eyes. In her they were wide, blue, clear eyes without a speck of age in them. She was beautiful, too, and her legs showing from under the blanket had not a single visible vein or scar. They were the legs of a woman of childbearing age. She closed her eyes when she saw us and seemed to shrink into herself. Then she opened them again and stared at me. She said something in a language I could not place. He told me it was Yiddish, Polish, German, Russian, and Spanish, all mingled together. She was trying to force us into sitting at the invisible dining table in the room and eating the chicken. He said something back to her in Yiddish. She stopped talking and stared at her son. A sigh came from her lips, a long trembling sigh like a moan. Then she looked at me again, her eyes moist with her suffering.

"Noe," she said.

She spoke her husband's name and reached for my hand.

"*Vamos*," she insisted, in Spanish now, almost in a whisper. "Let's go." He looked away.

Tears rolled slowly down along the bridge of her nose and disappeared into the corners of her mouth. I wanted to hug her, to take her away with me. I moved closer, but he asked me to step back. He took both of his mother's hands and held them tight in his. Hunched among pillows, her gray hair standing wildly on end, she began talking to herself, splitting into a number of quarreling selves. She seemed to be presiding over a meeting of many interested parties whose views she tried to reconcile. But the noisy meeting dissolved into curses.

He held her hands until an almost monastic calm reigned over her gray, bowed head. I stood in a corner paralyzed. Who we were and where we came from had never before felt to me more alien and separate than in this moment. I was lost in that room.

Later he and I walked through the streets of Manhattan. It had been a month since I left my father confounded in an airport. And in that time my teacher had semi moved in with me; his father had died; I had met his senile mother; I had betrayed him with someone else; I was pregnant again. We walked for hours, saying nothing. Late that night of January, we made love, also in silence.

I had not told him I was pregnant. I started to write as if it was something other than a child that was growing inside me. I waited and watched my body take over while my first book, the story of the two women in my life, began to find its way onto the page.

He had told me that family kills desire, not to mention love. A child at my age would turn me into one more gender casualty. He was thinking of me, shielding me from a woman's fate and the shackles of domestic life we all took on when the challenge of freedom seemed too much a burden to bear. I was pregnant with a child I wanted and knew he would despise. I was ignorant and uncultured and he was brilliant and smooth.

The days after we came back from New York City and before I was committed to a mental hospital, I rarely saw him. He had teaching work to catch up with and would soon come by, he said repeatedly on the phone. He met with his ex-wife several times to discuss their divorce documents and the fate of the boat and the house they had lived in for five years. I was convinced he had discovered the woman I truly was: too young, unstable, hollow, dumb, a problem, a burden.

My January rent was a month past due and so were the heat and phone bills. Father's money was never in the mail. Could I really be evicted? I stopped doing schoolwork and skipped classes four days in a row. I locked myself in the apartment unable to move. Without money any action seemed impossible. I was not accustomed to staying still. Doing nothing turned into a death wish that, frighteningly, seemed reasonable. The idea of being exposed to the man I loved, looking weak, worthless, and alone, plagued my thoughts. One day when all the windows in the apartment were frozen over and almost none of the gray light of day came through, I set the stage for a "proper" death with gas, pills, and alcohol. The landlord, who lived below me, brought down the theater curtain when he smelled the gas and called the firemen. I woke up to the hard knocks on the kitchen back door which led down to his apartment. Before he could come in, I picked myself up and literally ran the twelve blocks to the psychologist at the student medical center.

And here is where my other book comes in to inform this dark, spring semester of 1988, when at the end of this second visit to a psychologist I was told that I could make a phone call if I wished, but that according to the laws of the State of New York I couldn't leave the office. I was a threat to myself.

Surprisingly, he was there for me. He orchestrated, through physicians' friends, my transfer from the state mental hospital I was put in to a private one. He visited me every evening.

My father flew to Syracuse sometime in my first week at the hospital. The university dean for student affairs had called him. When I saw him walk into the visitor's room with my brother Fonso, I turned my back to them. To this day I still don't know why I did that, why turning my back to them, two men I loved, made me feel good, as if I was giving something back to them, as if they deserved it. When my father put his hand on my head and said, "You burned out, didn't you?" I felt him as alien and separate from me as I had felt toward the man I loved only weeks before at the old people's home. My father insisted I fly back to Puerto Rico with him for a semester's break, but I refused. I convinced him I could continue a few courses on an independent basis from the hospital. The dean had told me I could. He flew back home the next day saying he would come back soon. But he never did. I made sure of that.

I spent my days reading books my master brought me (and I hid from my therapist, who preferred I didn't read much during therapy): Julio Cortázar's *Rayuela*, Carlos Fuentes's *Aura*, Macedonio Fernández's *No todo es vigilia la de los ojos abiertos*, Bertrand Russel's *The History of Western Philosophy*, almost all of philosophers Martin Buber's and Walter Benjamin's and psychologists Melanie Klein's and Donald Winnicott's work, and the one book I treasured above all, André Schwarz-Bart's *The Last of the Just*. I worked hard at learning how to speak to him, how to listen, how to be worthy of the attention he was bestowing on me. I filled out endless series of 3 × 5 cards with annexations from the books I read. These cards lay everywhere in the room and grotesquely shrouded my cowardice. I would never be enough or have enough to repay him for including me in his life. He talked about boats, ocean crossings, and books to be written in the peace of an anchored life. That was why there could be no children or family for him. He had lots to do and little time.

Because you are young, he said again and again, *your life is just beginning, and you shouldn't be with me if you can't embrace the choices I've made in mine.*

I took his bluntness for a grand show of care, a sublime honesty, no matter if his freedom shone against the paleness of my character and the walls of my prison. But I wasn't totally in denial. The pregnancy was both a death sentence and a chance to rise above it, and above him.

With each week that went by during the hospital stay I noticed new changes in my body. My breasts swelled and gave off heat. He commented on my flushed cheeks and bright appearance. His comments were often followed by a caress. Once, he stared at me while his hand cupped my breast and I was sure he knew and was about to ask. He didn't. What he did ask was if I wanted to spend the summer break with him on his sailboat. For that, he said, I needed to make sure I was free. I could swear he was talking about ending the pregnancy.

I anguished over telling him. Time was running out to do anything but take it to term. I was somewhere between ten and twelve weeks along. My belly was growing and I wasn't eating much.

I looked through a book about pregnancy a nurse had given me, studying the picture of a fetus. I read that at fourteen to seventeen weeks, the fetus could suck his or her thumb, swallow amniotic fluid and pass it as urine, and make practice-breathing movements. I had to put the book away.

It was a Saturday at the end of March when I left the hospital with a backpack on each arm. He was in New York City attending a conference. The campus was deserted. I stared at the meaningless stream of cars going by, my brain as empty as the sidewalks. Outside the hospital ward, my restlessness and fear quickly gave way to hopelessness, a genuine hopelessness, when faith has evaporated and life seems to come to a standstill. I told myself to keep moving, that things would be just fine as long as I kept on moving.

I headed uphill toward the center of campus, sure that things would be okay. And they were, for just as I walked across the quad toward my apartment on the south side, the sun broke from behind the clouds. Bright rays caught the golden roof of Hendricks Chapel and slipped down along the long stone walls and the massive front steps until they reached my feet and the whole ground shone with radiance. I was engulfed in a feeling of absolute freedom and possibilities. I felt I was capable of doing whatever I wanted, of being whomever I wanted. When I looked at other people, I saw them without being worried about how they were seeing me. I was fine. I was pregnant. I was going to be a mother.

But then, just as suddenly as it came, the feeling disappeared. He would leave me when I told him I was having this baby. Each time the thought came to me I told myself I had to abort, but at that resolution my chest contracted and I gasped for air. I couldn't. I couldn't abort. I began to feel dizzy. I headed for a bathroom in the Architecture School building, nearly running. When I got there, I sat on the toilet cover. I felt like I was being pursued.

By the time I got to my apartment I was excited again to see him. I cleaned, did the laundry, organized my clothes, and made a grocery list. I walked by the phone and stared at it, as if the fact that it had not rung was a defect of the apparatus. Just as I began to panic, it rang. His voice was upbeat and he said he was only three hours away from Syracuse and would arrive with Chinese food. I rushed to the mini market down the street and bought a frozen Sara Lee pound cake for dessert and a lemon. I bathed, dressed, put on makeup and sat waiting for him with Oliveira at the kitchen table, the only furniture in the apartment beside the bed. I sucked on the lemon to quench my nausea. It was the only thing that helped.

Oliveira was a miniature Schnauzer who had been found hungry and cold on campus, trying to get into the school of Arts & Sciences. A student had given the lost eight-week-old puppy to him for an afternoon, but never came back, so he had brought Oliveira to the apartment. Oliveira was skittish from the beginning. When

I opened a plastic bag, he ran for cover under the kitchen table. Throughout his life, he would do the same with shower curtains, garbage bags, food wrappings, and raincoats. Sometimes, when the wind was right, the rustle of tree leaves would make him shiver. He was happiest being left alone. He ate, hardly touching his muzzle to the food. He never barked his distress. Even during the first nights, when he was merely a few months old, he simply sat on the floor at the foot of the bed, staring at us and shaking.

Over dinner, he congratulated me on my "rite of passage." The hospital was in the past now and I could move forward with my life. He asked if I would be ready to leave for the summer by the end of the following week, after final exams. Of course I would be ready, I said. I only needed to figure out my finances. As I said this, and as ashamed as I was of having said it, I hoped he would tell me not to worry about money, that he would take care of it. Though my father had paid the rent for the months I was hospitalized and had deposited a few hundred dollars in my bank account, I knew he was in financial trouble. I didn't know how I could explain to him a summer away from Puerto Rico. He had no idea of my current relationship beyond the craziness of that New Year's Eve day when I begged him to fly me back to Syracuse because I was in love. And if he expected me to be home anytime, it was now, this summer, out of a mental hospital. Just before my release my father had asked me for the dates I could fly home.

I saw the chopsticks come down to rest on the plate's side, and heard him stretching his back in the chair.

"Irenita," he said, "money is a delicate issue, but, truly, a symbolic one."

He crossed his arms and looked at me with what seemed a tender smile.

"I don't want to step into the father role. It's important that you keep your independence and remain a free woman."

I felt defeated.

Weeks went by. Early one morning, lying in bed, I realized that what I thought was gas was a small, minute motion. As faint as it was, I knew it was proof of the life within me and of the history we were becoming. Over dinner the same day, we sat on the porch drinking vodka. He told me again why he was attracted to me. It wasn't that I was young. It was true that the women he had been with were young, an average of twenty years younger, but the reasons were phenomenological and not psychological. He fell in love with us because we had no scars. Age for him was scar tissue, bitterness, inflexibility, an inability to go on the road. Women his age were riddled with worries and wounds. His brain and spirit shrunk in the company of those women. With me he felt he could travel, breathe in the evening air without dreading the bedroom. Curiously enough, his four previous wives had all suddenly wanted to be mothers when they hit their late twenties. He had not changed. They had changed.

Listening to him speak, I felt vertigo and just as some vertigo victims do at great heights, I took a leap. Walking to the opposite side of the porch, as far away from him as I could, I said I had something to tell him. I did.

Halfway through my confession he began nodding his head in agreement and he kept doing this after I was done talking. He added a *Sí, sí* . . . here and there until he finally stood up, put his hands deep in the pockets of his pants and, looking into my eyes, told me the choice was mine, only mine. I could choose to submit to fear and assume a life of motherhood and domesticity. He preferred I didn't. He saw potential in me. He quoted women, feminist thinkers and authors, to support his position.

"Is it my age?" I asked. "Am I too young to be a mother?"

"Not really. I would tell you the same thing if you were thirty. But then again, if you were alone or with a different man your choice would mean something else. If you are with me, you have to endure the burden of freedom, and that requires, in part, remaining childless. If you are grown up enough to have a child, you are just as fit to be a single mother. But I will not be a victim of your displacement."

I tried hard to recall what displacement meant, to understand what exactly I was making him a victim of. Before I had a chance to think or say anything further, he said he had to leave. At the door, he asked how long I'd known I was pregnant.

"I'm not sure," I told him, and watched him go down the stairs and out the door. What I feared most was happening right then and not in my head.

What comes next is difficult to tell. I stood in the middle of an empty room unable to think of anything but how to get him back, wavering between the piercing need to make a move and the dread of never moving again. I had no future other than being in this man's life. I had to make an appointment for an abortion. I didn't have a choice. I repeated this to myself over and over as I finally crawled into bed, overcome by a wave of fatigue, but not before swallowing once again the entire contents of a bottle of Tylenol and half a packet of Benadryl.

In the morning I woke to a stomachache. I itched all over. In the bathroom I noticed a dark-purplish rash covering most of my chest and arms. Some spots I must have scratched overnight were bleeding. Bending over the sink, a pang of nausea and dizziness sent me to the bathroom floor. I had to call the doctor's office. I just had to. Then I had to call him and say I had made a choice. I was not going to be a coward. I was going on the boat with him. I called.

I sat at the kitchen table and was sucking on a slice of lemon when I heard him knock. He was cheerful and funny and lifted me up when I opened the door. He was proud of my decision, he said, and asked how much packing I had to do to get ready for our trip. My mood began to lift. I cooked an egg-white omelet with his help and served him. Just as I set the plate down in front of him, I felt a painful cramp in my lower abdomen and back, and the urgent need to go to the bathroom. I didn't make it to the toilet. Halfway there I soiled myself. The diarrhea ran down my legs under my short nightgown and reached the floor. Oliveira ran to my feet and licked my toes.

He then looked up from the table and at that second a wrenching jab forced me to hold on to the wall before the gushing water covered my miniature schnauzer in blood. I recall apologizing on a stretcher near a hospital laundry room ashamed by the screams of pain I could not hold back. I recall excusing myself to people passing by. There was a woman doctor who at one point pushed my stretcher down a long corridor and into a room and then disappeared between my legs. I recall the surprise at seeing her big pregnant belly popping into view between us, her blond hair held tight in a bun on top of her head.

As she fought to get her own seven- or eight-month pregnant belly out of the way, I pitied her, in the English sense of the word. She backed up, straightened out her lab coat, sighed and looked at me with the same pity. There, in a version of pity born out of disgust and guilt rather than compassion, we were in unison.

After a while, she pushed the stretcher back to the same spot in the hallway and left me there without a word. I remember the pained face of my friend Alba and how it turned severe when he appeared. He said they were trying to get my gynecologist to the hospital as soon as possible. He said he had to give his last seminar and would be back after four hours. He said other things, too, but I could barely make out his words through the contractions that were by then constant.

I didn't know they were contractions. I didn't know my cervix was quickly dilating at 5 centimeters, and that the ultrasound had shown its length at 23 centimeters. I didn't know I was being left to dilate naturally, that since the fetus was not a viable fetus, the hospital staff felt they could wait for my doctor to show up while I labored in the hallway. The only thought in my mind was when would the pain go away. At one point, I looked for him and he was gone and so was Alba.

When I woke in the operating room, Dr. N, the physician who had performed my first abortion, had both hands fastened to my cheeks. He was calling my name and demanding I look into his eyes. His arms were shaking considerably and it took some time to see I was the one trembling. I wouldn't come out from under the anesthesia. I had lost too much blood and my body temperature had fallen to deadly levels. An evacuation on my second-trimester pregnancy had been performed to complete the inevitable abortion and stop the hemorrhage that had finally called the attention of the staff to my gurney. I had almost died.

In the recovery room an angry and bereft Dr. N asked me why. When I said "Why what?" he threw his arms in the air and yelled: "Why on earth would you get pregnant within a month of the first abortion?" and "Who on earth would wait so long to do something about it? Because," and he brought his face close to mine, "you can't fool me." I had done something to end my pregnancy; he had way too many years in the profession. He was among the first doctors to offer abortions in upstate New York. He believed in women's right to abort, but he had seen it all. Had I any idea that I was only two weeks from a premature birth? At eighteen weeks, my abortion was medically a late miscarriage, but to him there was no difference between an eighteen-week fetus and a twenty-week one. He had collected close to 480 grams of fetal body weight. Five hundred grams of fetal body weight is considered a viable fetus. I had risked my life for no reason and had come awfully close to ending that of an infant.

"Don't listen to the doctor," I said to him sitting at the foot of the bed. He had a hand on my foot and squeezed it gently. "I should have taken birth control as I told you I had."

I could hear Dr. N in the hallway speaking to a nurse. He sounded as worked up as when he had asked me, boldly, if the grown man by my side was the father of the child I had miscarried. I did not have to respond because Dr. N left the room mumbling. At the door he turned and angrily asked the man I loved if he didn't know what a condom was.

I had aborted a pregnancy I wanted, had almost died, and all I could feel was terror at becoming a man's problem. I struggled to find an explanation, something to make him understand I wasn't a mess, that I could do something right, after all, something to put his life at ease so he could finally write the books his women kept him away from. As I apologized and confessed about the pills I had taken the night before, I could see his face relax and his eyes close a bit with pity and understanding. His hand reached for my chin and pinched it softly while the other slid under my hospital gown and cupped a breast. He said something along these lines:

"You are stronger than I could ever imagine, Irene. People are and will always be threatened by our story. Here, this breast of yours in my hand is to wipe out everything that is not us. Forget the hospital, your doctor, and the fantasies to give birth to somebody else for fear of having to birth your own self. A big project begins here for you today. You have a mother and grandmother's suicidal fantasies to break free from. I'm going to help you. What you have is a beautiful problem, it's what poetry is made of, so don't feel bad my young Alfonsina. I'm going to show you the ocean and you'll see how everything painful shrinks at the horizon."

When he said "young Alfonsina" his voice broke almost imperceptibly, enough for me to sense the great feeling passing through him. Alfonsina Storni was an Argentinean writer who one day, just like Virginia Woolf, walked into a death by water. It was a slightly new side of him I was witnessing but suspected; he had a weakness for sadness and tragedy and women at the brink of self-annihilation. It was a weakness I would learn to exploit to perfection, one that involved the romantic and modernist traditions embedded in our Spanish language, which his Lacan and deconstructivism had not succeeded in purging. It was also a weakness nursed by the melancholy of exile and the extermination of most of his dearest friends at the hands of a dictatorship.

As much as he proclaimed the need to free me from my personal biography, it was this biography that made up much of his attraction to me. I can't know how conscious I was of this drama, but I know that by the time I was released from the hospital two days later, I felt more secure about him; I had more power. And I very quickly assumed an Alfonsina Storni persona. I became a writer tangled up in the giant octopus of family history and suicide so that he could only love me more. The pact was sealed. I didn't know a thing except that I must do all that was needed for him to love me.

The moment we got into his van to head for East Hampton, he started the engine, sat back, and stared at me. I asked if he had forgotten something, but he didn't answer and went on staring with a pensive look. Then he nodded his head as if he had solved a riddle. It made me nervous, this habit of his, of thinking and nodding to no one in particular.

He said that living on a boat for extended periods of time was perhaps the biggest test one could put on a couple. It was too easy to project onto the other what bothered us most about ourselves. The small space, the long hours empty of distractions, the silence of life at sea, the rationing of water and energy, all could be frustrating and frightening. Sailing tested your character, faced you with big challenges, and summoned the coward or the hero in you.

I listened, unsure of where he was going. Then he told me:

"You are going to have to write. There is no other way. I write every morning from seven to one and read in the afternoon. If I don't, the boat can feel like a prison. To protect the love for the boat and to protect the story between us, we each have to have something going besides sailing. You see, what one loves the most shouldn't become the center. You'll write while I work and we'll meet up at the end of the day. Yes, that will work. Just look at the two women in your life, the three of you are some Russian doll of self-destruction. There is a book there. You've just got to work hard. You'll have to learn to write." He went on nodding again to himself and drove away.

And learn is what I would set out to do. Learn to sail, learn to cook, learn to tend to him and the boat, learn to not think about the growing distance between me and my father and relatives, learn to forget the things I had cared for before meeting him, dear friends, God, graduate school, dance, dominoes, roasted pork, Wonder Bread. I don't think he actually believed I would learn to write. I for one was pretty sure I wouldn't. But the routine was set and I was more than happy to be of use, especially because of how destitute I felt, having to come up with excuses for my father's missing allowance. As for my father, I told him a half-truth. I was going sailing with Alba and the professor and then staying with Alba for some time. I promised I would fly back home at the end of the summer for a few weeks. I knew the missing checks were his way of saying he knew the truth.

When we arrived in East Hampton, we were invited to cocktails by old friends of his on the boat docked next to his *Sarabande*. A good number of couples were already sipping drinks on that gigantic sailboat. I went to take a shower in the marina's public restrooms, feeling cast away from this other world of his and as insignificant as the Mexican woman who was cleaning the bathrooms. I could not help gravitating toward this woman, asking her questions, killing time and finding in our Spanish language a refuge of sorts.

He came in just as I was handing her a bottle of Windex. It had been an hour since I was supposed to join him. He walked away and I followed, trying to catch up with him. As I went for the lifeline of the boat to pull myself on board, I fell in the water between the docks and the boat.

I could hear the laughter underwater. I touched the muddy bottom with my feet and my shoes sank in and stuck like glue. After I freed myself, I hesitated to go up. I hung around that muddy bottom until I was out of air. On the surface, I just floated, looking for him in the crowd gathered on the side of the boat. People were telling me to swim to the ladder behind me on the dock. As I turned, I could make out his blue satin shirt. He was sitting on a raft aft of the boat. I climbed out of the water and flashed a wet smile to everyone on board before heading back to the showers, wondering why on earth he had not given me a hand.

That night, lying in bed, he said there was no place for suicidal personalities on a boat. Sailing demanded one's full attention. It was a matter of responsibility. Other people's lives were at stake. My fall angered him and he couldn't afford to think of me as an unreliable young thing. If he started seeing me that way, it was the end of our story. He rolled over, an AM mini radio against his left ear.

Ashamed, I cried myself to sleep, but not before swearing I would prove to him he had not wasted his time in choosing me.

I got to work the next morning. By the end of July, two months later, *Sarabande* was the beauty of the harbor. The teak outside couldn't hold another layer of varnish and both the topside fiberglass and the hull sparkled under the sun. Every morning I buffed and polished the decks and every piece of stainless steel, including nuts and bolts. Down below I stripped all the spots in the teak with faded varnish or water stains and brought the wood back to matching perfection. My mouth tasted of sanded wood. I smelled of varnish and turpentine. No amount of showering could wash the smell off me.

On August 7, my nineteenth birthday, we anchored off Cutty Hunk. We had left two days earlier for our first trip, stopping on Block Island along the way. I was terrified of the ocean, pathetically seasick, restless to get to shore, certain we would crash and sink, and determined to not show a sign of my true state of body and mind. The seasickness was difficult to cover up and he had me look out at the horizon repeatedly to help with the nausea. It only made me sicker. But I told him he cured me.

It goes without saying that I was glad to arrive in Cutty Hunk, a charming little island where we planned to stay put for a few weeks before heading back to close up the boat for the fall and winter. Shortly after setting the anchor, I saw a dark, gray mass filling the sky, heading our way. He set out to secure the jib and asked me to furl tight the main sheet. This task was one of the few things he had taught me thoroughly. I felt competent at it. I was halfway done when the squall hit us. The wind changed direction drastically and whipped up, taking the topping lift halyard from my left hand. I saw the line go up high above the boat and then descend in circles wrapping itself perfectly around the top of the mast with only the end shackle loose and chiming against the sail track.

He stood next to me holding on to the gooseneck of the boom, looking up, and shaking his head. This was exactly the scenario he had talked about, when full attention and responsibility were summoned, with no leeway for spacing out. He had noticed I was up for an accident because I had broken two glasses in the last week, put toilet paper in the head instead of the basket, clogging it, and shown signs of falling ill.

"Irene, if you aren't comfortable on the boat be frank about it. Pretending otherwise simply to earn my approval is a manipulation bound to turn into an accident, just like this one." There was tenderness in his eyes mixed with exasperation. "If this happened at sea and we couldn't get up the mast, what would happen?"

As he was getting his bosun chair ready to go up the sixty-eight foot mast, he looked up at the sky and said it would not work. He could not trust me with winching him up. There was too much wind, he was heavy, and I could make a mistake and let go of the line. He had to call the marina on the island and ask for a rigger to come and charge us a fortune to untie the damn halyard.

I saw my salvation. It was as simple as going up myself and fixing the mess I had made. I would show him I could mend things. I could be trusted again with his life. He hesitated and then said the plan might work. The responsibility was on him to keep me safe, after all. He would tie a second safety line to the spreaders and all I had to do was guide myself, holding on to the mast with both hands and feet as he winched me up.

And up I went. A few feet from reaching the halyard, I remembered that I was afraid of heights. I told myself to not look down or ahead, but the thought of where I was made me dizzy and my stomach began to turn. I hugged the mast closer and wrapped my feet around it more than I should have. He felt the resistance below. It was too hard to continue winching me up. I yelled down that I needed a break, a few minutes that was all.

And in those few minutes I remembered many other things I shouldn't have at that moment, perched up on an aluminum rod sixty feet off the ground. I remembered I had missed my period in June and then again in July. I remembered I was four days late in August. I remembered I believed it had to do with the miscarriage, the surgery, and an irregular recovery period. I remembered I had been constantly nauseous for the past week, even when I was off the boat. I remembered his threat to leave if I had a child. I remembered Dr. N.

He called and I looked down. From up where I was the boat was a frighteningly small thing, the water all around a deadly, beautiful blue, and all of a sudden the dark, gray mass filling the sky was below me. I threw up.

Back in Syracuse, I took a bath and saw my stomach protruding through the bubbles, my hipbones invisible even lying flat. I sat up, sunk my body in the water out of sight. But there was no avoiding it. The memory came back to me. The day of that second abortion when Dr. N told me I had come close to ending the life of an infant; the blood on Oliveira; the stretcher by the dirty laundry room of the hospital; the contractions; the blond, pregnant doctor; Dr. N's anger. I feared it was too late. I called Mercedes. By the time she arrived I was terrified the man I loved would leave me for good and go back to his ex-wife.

Mercedes accompanied me to a new gynecologist in town, Dr. Y. I was too afraid to go back to Dr. N. She gave me the money for the procedure. In fact, she had paid for the first abortion. He would come to know of all the pregnancies, except for the first and third, which I told him about years later. He always said, "You know what I think." The abortion that took place in the emergency room was paid for by my student health insurance and by my father, who I believe never realized what the hospital bills had been for. He never asked either.

The academic year of 1988–1989 is mostly gone from my mind. I know I was pregnant again on the boat and that in late August, shortly after returning to Syracuse, I asked Alba what to do. She put her arms around me and said something was not right. Why didn't I move in with her and her parents, and rest, eat, sleep. She was worried about my weight and all the pregnancies. Three in less than a year, she reminded me.

My best friend was indeed the voice of reason, yet I stepped away from her embrace, rejecting her sensible offer, a bit annoyed at her measure and freedom. I had completely relinquished mine, how dare she flash hers at the walls of my prison? I seldom saw Alba for the rest of the month and for the rest of the decade. I turned away from anything or anybody that would see a flaw in my life with this man. And the same would happen with my father and my country. In the fifteen years between 1987 and 2002 I only went back home three times (1991, 1994, 2002), though my father found his quiet way to me a couple of times.

I spent most of September sitting in his bed attempting to write something worth showing him. Whenever he came out of his makeshift office in the walk-in closet, and saw me at my work, he would nod in approval and smile. My days were organized around that nod and that smile. It was all I longed for, and out of this overwhelming need of approval from him I disciplined myself day in and day out around a yellow notebook. Each time I heard Alba's voice on the answering machine I quickly, almost in panic, erased the message before letting myself hear it. One day in October I found myself taking the phone jack out of the wall. Just the thought of hearing her voice or that of my father or brothers or any other relative or friend was too unpleasant.

I tried to ignore the changes in my body. Yet, once in a while, I locked myself in the bathroom leafing through the pregnancy book I still had. I calculated that I was in my third month. The fact that the nausea had let up after two months and that clothes were too tight around my waist and bust, told me I must have gotten pregnant in late May.

The drawings in "The Third Month" chapter showed a fetus three inches long and two ounces in weight, about the size of an apple. Taste buds were developed and fingers and toes had soft nails covering them. The heartbeat could be heard with a Doppler. I felt simultaneously a shudder of happiness and a chilling terror sitting on the toilet with the book on my lap, ultimately having to close it and hide it away in despair. One morning I called Dr. Y's office and left a message with the receptionist. He probably returned my call, but the phone must have been disconnected. Another day, I called Planned Parenthood and made an appointment I didn't keep. I called Mercedes, Alba's mother, for advice, but after we exchanged greetings I couldn't make myself speak. She said to wait while she fetched Alba. I said I had to run to the bathroom. I would call right back. I never did.

Finally we went to New York City for five days. The first night there, he found out that his ex-wife Ada was pregnant. His NYU friend, whose place we were staying in, told us the news in passing as he was leaving for the airport. He and his friend had been talking about the importance of not having children and staying loyal to their writings. The friend, in his late forties, was engaged to get married the following month for the first time and had included this condition in his marriage agreement.

After his friend left, he went to the kitchen and got a bottle of wine. He said we had to celebrate. He had escaped Ada's fate. He was happy. And as for her, well, she thought she was happy, and what was the difference. "Who cares!" he said, winking as he handed me a wineglass. What mattered was that he was free, he was with me, and I, his courageous little woman, was intent on being as free as he was. He was very proud of me. My life would be something I would look back at late in my years without regrets. Ada had joined the ranks of the cowards. Ada was going to be a mother by Christmas. I was going to abort my third pregnancy.

On the morning of our second day in Manhattan, while he was out with friends, I opened the yellow pages and searched for abortion clinics. Each one I called had too many protocols, preventing the termination from taking place before our departure in three days. In desperation, I explained my situation to a receptionist who referred me to a clinic. I called and made an appointment for the next day.

I walked into the clinic fearing this one would do me in. Like the miscarriage, it was a second-trimester abortion. The Haitian doctor sat me down and explained the procedure. At sixteen to seventeen weeks, the fetus was too big for a dilation and curettage. I had to go through a two-day abortion that entailed overnight dilation and evacuation of the womb the following day. She told me I had to watch a movie. I begged her not to make me watch it. She handed me a folder and asked me to read instead. Details about the procedure and recovery were explained inside. I threw it in the garbage the moment she closed the door behind her.

The doctor warned me: a girl who keeps on doing this to herself is bound for a pact with the devil. Yet, amidst the rancor that I could sense in her hands as she pushed one laminaria needle after another against the walls of my cervix, a quiet pity in her eyes almost lulled me to sleep. I begged for pity in the Spanish sense of the word, *piedad*, which means looking frantically for a sign of sorrow in the other's eyes, sorrow for another's suffering. I never saw it in myself, not even in the mirror, for such was the poverty of my spirit.

That night, bent over by cramps, my cervix dilating, I watched *Casablanca* for the first time. I was waiting for him to come back from dinner with friends, praying he would stay out longer. He walked in just when, toward the end of the movie, Captain Louis Renault throws a bottle of Vichy water against the floor, condemning with this gesture an occupied France and sealing his friendship with Bogart. He replayed that scene several times, trying to explain the beauty of that moment of truth, until, realizing that I was in pain, he gave up and helped me into bed.

I lay in bed staring at a show poster for *A Chorus Line*. In the dark, the backdrop glowed, almost with a purpose. Between my legs there was a bag of ice and I was counting one girl, two girls, and so on, each of them breathing in a contraction for me. I did it quietly, so he wouldn't hear and the dilating laminaria needles the clinic inserted earlier that morning wouldn't fall out. I believed in his notion that writing can turn shit into gold. My pain and the death springing within me were working material. Beyond that, I did not exist. This belief allowed, among other things, for a second-trimester fetus to be as disposable as I was. At some moment, staring at that musical poster, I felt I got it all right and jumped out of bed to jot down in my brand new writer's journal: "Must see *A Chorus Line*." I looked at the sleeping man who had given me the diary and was grateful.

Later, hearing me moan in my sleep, he asked what was wrong. I told him I had a cyst, nothing serious, and that I had an appointment the next day to remove it. The pain I was feeling had me a little careless with words. I saw the truth and the judgments coming, but they didn't. Instead, he grabbed my right hand and put it on his chest. He told me about his dinner with the art dealer Holly Solomon, about the possibility for him as an art critic to curate a group show at the Stedlijk museum in Amsterdam in two years. The title he was thinking of was "American Baroque." What did I think of when I heard that title, "American Baroque" . . . ?

Half conscious from pain, I answered with a question: would you lend me some money to pay the clinic? My father has yet to send me a check. I fell asleep counting girls off the poster.

Over breakfast I promised that he would not to have to wait too long for me to come back. He had looked up from the *New York Times* and I could almost see a glimpse of worry in his eyes, but then again, the arts section had a picture of the Argentinean writer J. L. Borges. It was the end of an era, he said, his teachers were dying, and this one, in particular, dead now for two years, felt more like the country itself had died.

I never knew what happened to me during the abortion or to the fetus I carried. A man with emphysema had limped his way to me, gasping for air, introduced himself as the doctor and asked if I was allergic to any medication. I looked into his eyes, begging, but there was nothing there, only lack of air. I was told anesthesia was being administered and that when I woke up, all would be over. It wasn't.

A young man blocked my way out of the clinic. He asked if I was scheduled to come back the next morning. I couldn't understand what he meant. Two older men and a woman joined us and told him they had seen me the day before. Then it dawned on me, the placards in their hands said it all. I tried to walk past them, but the woman took me by the arm, saying she would pray for my soul and that of the child I had killed.

I kept writing and busied myself with books and index cards through the long winter. He worked on his novel. When we met up at meal times we mostly spoke of plans to sail the boat south to the Bahamas in the summer. It was a fantasy that organized our days, just as much as the abortions did. In February of 1990 I went back to Dr. Y for a fifth termination.

It took a while but a time came when I welcomed the writing job he had asked me to do. The shift occurred after I read Simone de Beauvoir's *Memoirs of a Dutiful Daughter.* There was something that shook me profoundly about the intimate picture of a young woman growing up in a suffocating world and striking out on her own with such existential ambition that even a mother's death becomes a footnote to her story. As I became more involved with my book, he began to fight hard to keep my identity in check. Each time I wrote a memory down, he reminded me of Paul de Man and the death of autobiography. "I" would always remain an ideological construct, and so a fiction of sorts. I was never to believe in the importance of what I was doing beyond the practicality of writing a book that organized our common schedule and could potentially bring us money. As for me, I was to embark on a writing life to create a cohesive whole I could live with, ignorant that what I amplified and allowed to recede through the quiet sleight of hand that were his edits of my work, would become a life I could not live with.

Hegel said: The truth is the whole, but spirit gains its truth by finding itself in dismemberment.

In the published book there is no promiscuous teenager shaming her way through Mexico, or in love with her literature professor, bowing her way through life for fear of looking it in the face and seeing it for what it is, a room where you are, ultimately, all alone. There are no abortions either, except for a "miscarriage" mentioned in passing at the end. Instead, the memoir follows a college girl coming undone as the mourning for her mother catches up with her. Pressures from the adult world that include underperforming in college, splitting with a boyfriend, the burden of an adolescent body, depression, and the progressive slowing down into inertia are narrated in broad terms, in passing. Only the suicide attempts are given in detail, but even these are lacking an identifiable referent that inspired them. It's as if the movement toward self-annihilation was happening in a vacuum, the vacuum of a history attractive enough in its tragic sense to be understood as the reason for it all. My misery at the center of the book is historically romanticized, and the personal, domestic truths of a self's struggles are for the most part missing.

The book pretended to be the whole truth but there was much more to tell. I was trapped in a false self, unable to tell the bigger story.

I wrote in that book:

As I entered the hospital I was far from knowing the reasons for my sadness. Many times, faint at the very sight of a clock's hands turning past the hour, I would sink sideways into my chair, clinging to the second that had just elapsed. It was as if the time had come and I was sum-moned to answer.

Today I know that you aren't ignorant of your sadness when that sadness has put you in a mental hospital for trying to kill yourself. You might feel disoriented, confused, but you do know the immediate reasons that led you there. And in my case it was no cute clock ticking away life, nor was it only my grandmother's attack on the U.S. Congress thirty-something years earlier, or my mother's suicide when I was a child. I know today my suicide at-tempts were due to my destructive efforts to banish the awareness of my impotence, my fear of the outside world, through a man who could not offer me the safety I had searched for all my life. All seven suicide attempts took place when we were together (two in 1988, one in 1989, three in 1993, and one in 1995). I cloaked myself in the shadow of the power he represented, hoping to not look weak, worthless. But it did not protect my self-esteem or chase away the anxiety gnawing at me.

I should have written:

As I entered the hospital, I was certain I would carry the second pregnancy to term. I tried to not think about what he would have to say, when and if he found out. Each time I failed to keep my fears out of my mind, I quickly took refuge in the fantasy of single motherhood but each time the fear of losing him wrecked everything. I slept my anguish away and welcomed the medication a nurse brought into my room three times a day.

He had told me: "Your mother's death was your salvation. You should be thankful she died."

On the last page of the book, I wrote that my mother's death was not necessarily my doom but my redemption. I went on with this crooked thought in a convoluted paragraph about phenomenology.

. . . Mother has died, therefore I am, I wrote. *Not a nation, it is true, but a presence that remains. A book.*

That my mother's death could have redeemed me, what an ill thought and how romantic. The idea was his.

I was writing for him, you see.

I quiet the shame of my half-truths by reminding myself that all the provisional selves that seem to be my true makeup don't have to be reason for despair. I've despaired enough. I only need to navigate them, their ambiguities and contradictions, as I write this "truer" account down. My task is not only with memory but with tackling an older narrator's relationship with a younger aspect of self. This younger self that I am and am no longer must give up her idealized memory and somehow share her house with her older sibling, "I."

As I look back, I'm struck by the ordinariness of my suicide attempts and the stupidity orchestrating my emotions. The realization scares me as much as it angers me.

One day in late March 1990, I walked aimlessly through campus for hours, returning to our apartment after dusk. The next day I started an affair.

James Merton had been one of my professors during freshman year when I took his class on Critical Religion. I was still reading books on adoption that second college semester when average C grades kept on piling up. A disquieting anonymity followed me to class and back to my dorm. My grades and social isolation slowed me down. When James handed me a final paper with a big, blue *A* written across my name, I fell in love with him. Soon Ivan came along and took care of the rest. And I forgot about James.

In that strange fall semester after Mexico when I began my relationship with my professor, I took another course with James on Rhetoric of Religion. Though we seldom met aside from class and lunches here and there, I knew him as an extremely gentle and caring man who showed admiration and respect for me. When I was hospitalized and allowed to take one independent study to not lose touch with college, it was James whom I turned to. The other A grade he gave me on that independent study, while I was an inpatient at a mental hospital, stuck with me as one of the most proud, pleasurable moments in my entire life. I did not fall in love with him again, but I could not have been more grateful. Now, in 1990, I was trying to wrap up my BA with eighteen credits and asked him for a waiver to register in his graduate class on Alfred North Whitehead.

Our affair began one evening during a class gathering at a bar. I kept on spacing out and could not follow the questions directed at me. I looked out the window often to see if I would catch my man with his ex-wife. Her office in the psychology department was across the street from the university hotel. The day before, I had found her at his office, sitting on the edge of his desk, bending over his manuscript and reading from it aloud in her quiet, Argentinean voice. She smiled at me and slowly stood up, all the while looking at him, and saying something about tango. Then she walked out of the room, with her petite ballerina, thirty-year-old body, glancing at me once and staring at my ridiculous snow hat. Afterward, he and I argued about finances. Where was my father's check for the rent and for my semester's books? He had a way of bringing up the subject as if it were a puzzle to him that my father was irresponsible, leaving his daughter at the mercy of an unequal relationship with a man. I told him I needed to go to the library. Instead I walked aimlessly through campus feeling worthless.

When James called me aside from the gathering and asked if something was wrong, I said I'd just had my fifth abortion. Later that night, in his bed, he hugged me tight and asked me to marry him. I said I couldn't leave the man I was with. He answered: I know.

Our affair continued for three weeks. He asked me several times to move in with him. A most unpossessive man, he was a bachelor at forty-eight, a suffering, brilliant, tragic thinker, struggling to overcome his own addiction to alcohol. His days revolved around writing—he had produced ten books—and teaching, for which he won awards. He symbolized a safe base.

He said he had fantasized about marrying me before, but that I had been too young. Now I was twenty. He knew I lived with another man, a good man and colleague of his, but if that relationship ever ended, he wished I would give him a chance. I was moved and flattered. I told him I loved the man I lived with. I told him I valued his friendship. I liked the woman I turned into when I talked with him. I was direct, frank, and fearless.

Through those guilt-ridden weeks of the affair, I confided in Mercedes. She listened with almost passionate attention, refilled her chocolate Vienna drink too often, began a habit of lighting up a cigarette with one still going out in the ashtray, and sent me off at the end of the evening with the same warning:

"Do not ever tell, even in a moment of guilt-ridden weakness. He will never understand and will only make your life miserable for the rest of your time together. This had to happen. Don't do anything drastic. Don't do anything. Let it run its course. You listen to me, yes? You are not in love with James. You love the man you live with. And yes, he has a few things to learn if he doesn't want to lose you. At some point you have to tell him what you'd like him to do differently. Now you just don't know. But you are on your way to finding out."

One evening I found James drunk at the university hotel bar, which he frequented. Mia, a PhD student, was holding his head on her lap. When he saw me he laughed a hollow laugh while his hands flung about trying to straighten up his body. Food clung to the corners of his mouth. He looked up at me with dull, glassy eyes I could see my white shirt reflected in.

• • •

Sometime in April I went to Holland. Holly Solomon, the New York gallery owner, had finally hired him to curate an art exhibit.

In Amsterdam I felt smaller and more insignificant than ever. At every gathering, I was seated far away from him while other couples were placed together. Holly Solomon made some of those decisions; other times, he told me where to sit. One night, lying in bed looking out the window at a full moon, I felt unhappy. Several days later, we were having lunch with a close artist friend of his, and as of recently mine, when she asked what was up with us. He acted surprised. I didn't. She pointed her fork at me while looking at him and said: "You won't give this woman a child and you won't marry her. You're about to lose her."

Later, back in Syracuse, I was working late on my application to graduate school. He came into the room and sat on the floor by my chair. He grabbed my ankle. He caressed it. I looked down at him, surprised at the tenderness. Then he asked if I would marry him and sail around the world.

Finally, I knew what to do with my life.

The summer of heading south arrived. We were to sail the boat to Virginia and then to the Bahamas. We would go through the Intracoastal Waterway and exit to the ocean twice for overnight passages. He watched me pack three months of provisions and praised my spirit of adventure. My industriousness amused him. I had learned to care for a boat the previous summer. Now I could organize our lives in it, even captain it if the occasion came. He had begun to need me. I was elated and empowered by my growth.

East Hampton swarmed with convertibles and fine young ladies who smiled their way past me. They smelled good, too. I felt so broke and inadequate in my faded jeans and old shoes. I was basically living off him. My college stipend had shrunk considerably since my father found out that we were living together. It happened over Christmas when he wanted me to fly home as I had done every holiday. I stumbled over absurd reasons to not go. He finally asked me directly if I was living with the teacher and if I was going to spend Christmas with him. The lease of the apartment I had rented the previous fall had ended too, and I was running out of excuses to tell him. He still sent me money but much less and irregularly. The "teacher" picked up the bill, of course, but we kept track of the half I owed, for when the money came in, so that I could go on living up to the "free" woman status he wanted. Being twenty that summer felt like twelve.

With the change from the money he gave me for groceries I looked for something to buy. Shopping always lifted my spirits. Anything would do. I went into the first store that seemed afford-able. There was a table filled with used books on sale for a dol-lar. I picked up one that had a picture of a small sailboat on the cover, a true story of a seventeen-year-old who sails around the world, and another that had a drawing of a sweet little girl hold-ing a frightened pig. I had no idea what it was about, but the table of contents had appealing headings such as Escape, Lone-liness, Summer Days, Bad News, the Miracle, Last Day, A Warm Wind . . . There was also a tiny spider hanging from the title, *Charlotte's Web*.

I took these two books. They lay next to me in bed all through-out the summer and a dream began to take shape. Feeling like that little pig Wilbur, cushioned by little Fern's compassion, and driven by the wits and courage of that large, gray spider, Charlotte A. Cavatica, I jumped into the little sailboat of the other book and went around the world. Few times have I felt as rich and in need of nothing as when I read those books. Soon after, we began our sunset ritual of sitting on the cockpit over gin and tonic and jot-ting down things we needed to get so we could cast off and head south. The lists and tasks filled my days and evenings.

The morning of our departure I woke up to the words "Let's go" and a shine in his eyes that made me look out the hatch. A light breeze rippled the surface of the water. Above, the sky was scrubbed with wind and the clouds were racing by. The air in my face was cooling and it entered me and filled me with hope.

What I did not expect was the panic of emotion that swamped me at the onset of the long trip south to the Bahamas. I was not only afraid of the wind and the sea. I was afraid of the boat. I was afraid of reefing the sails, or putting them up, or changing them in any way. I was afraid of stopping the engine, afraid of starting it again. I was so afraid whenever a ship appeared, I could not take my eyes off her until she vanished.

I still feel the terror spreading from my eyes down my spine to the tip of my toes. The first day he instructs me to let the line go the minute he tells me. While I wait for his sign, he backs the twenty-ton sailboat out of the dock. The same wind that is pushing those clouds up above way too fast wants to do the same with us. He yells through the wind to hold fast but I hear let go. He runs up and down the deck. He pulls up the sails. I sit stiff and frozen behind the steering wheel he's asked me to only hold in position, that's all. We miss crashing into every single object by mere inches, the lobster boat, the docks, the pump station, the flagpole, the ferry, the child fishing off the dinghy, his fisherman grandfather fending us off. I keep my eyes fixed on the shore. The sailboat rocks dangerously. The mast creaks. By slight jerks the marina and the dock and the people on it get smaller and smaller and the sounds of land grow clearer, more distinct. A dense cold rises all around sending shivers across my skin. A gust of wind fills the sail. We fly across the bay and the joy of being on the water takes a seat next to my terror.

The first day out was memorable because of the fog. A steamer loomed up astern and took my breath away before sheering off to starboard and disappearing. I spent the night in clammy discomfort in the cockpit expecting to be run down any moment by another boat. In the late afternoon of the second day, the wind backed up. It began to blow from the northeast. *Sarabande* was flying, her boom way out and lifting, tugging at the mainsheet. Her mainsail, taut and straining, was a wing against the high sky. And when dusk came, the night sky was filled with glittering stars.

My numbness wore off very slowly. The first few days passed in a frightened haze he never suspected and which the entries in my logbook omitted. These entries were mainly recordings of times, wind and sea conditions. I don't remember actually going to sleep during those first days when we set out from Three Mile Harbor down Long Island Sound and into the Atlantic Ocean, though I must have done so. I do remember feeling so tired that my only ambition was to curl up and sleep for a week.

I had never before set foot on a boat except for the cruise ship I went on for my high school graduation, but the discovery of sailing remains among the most authentic and empowering experiences of my adult years. The woman I was and kept on becoming each time I faced a challenge on the sea kept me afloat throughout years of depression and self-mutilation. At sea I lived in a world of finite size and finite human acts. The world was the length of that boat and the sphere of human action was everything I did in it. Each act took on huge proportions, tying a knot in a line, plotting a sextant shot, resting for several hours before a night watch. Any act could set off a chain of events ending in death. If that knot at the end of the mainsheet was not right you would lose the sail, maybe the boat itself if the waves tipped you over and the wind pushed the hull against the rocks.

The sea was a vast field of waves. At night it spoke with such terrible beauty and profound indifference that when you finally reached land you wanted to get as far away from it as you could. You ran off, even staying at a hotel in town while paying for dockage at the marina, only to yearn for it soon after. There was a perversion to the whole thing. You cast off to arrive at port. You tie up to cast off.

I loved those moments when the silence was like a sound in itself. At the end of the day during those first sailing trips I found myself exploring coves, looking for the best one to protect the boat from the wind and the waves. I finally dropped anchor and let out plenty of chain, backing down to get the flukes deep into the sand. I studied tide tables over cocktails to make sure I had enough scope so that even if the wind found the boat, the anchor would hold. Before going to bed I took bearings against the shore to check later if the boat drifted or was swinging safely. I slept lightly at night. The boat moved, swinging with the current, and I ran terrified to deck convinced that my hand would reach the shore. Every time I would find *Sarabande* rocking freely to a passing wake. It all depended on you, not on God, but on you. If you didn't bury those flukes deep enough, if you didn't calculate the direction of the current, or let out enough chain, you could end up in the rocks. One day would follow another in that anchored life, months at a time.

I came to know that I was ever ready to balance on a floor that pitches and rolls, to gaze at a flat horizon that, at any moment, a sudden wind or wicked current might turn into a rocky shore. I came to know all my senses could adjust time after time. They could respond to the surface texture of the water, the smoothness or chop of the seas, the feel of the wind, the smell of the air, even the shape of the foam riding the cresting waves. I came to know firsthand of something that would stay forever with me through this day: I was resilient.

Oliveira and I saw the sun rise and set most days in the years aboard the boat. It would be the two of us in an eleven-foot inflatable dinghy on the way to or from the half-moon sandy beach he loved to dig his nose in. It would be me watching him stand on the minute bow of the boat, his nose twisted this way and that toward the beach as we approached. Each year he grew more confident of his acrobatic moves on that bow, so that one season, at the first sight of the beach and a quarter mile or so from it, he lined up his body with the side of the inflatable, spread his paws and launched himself into the sea. When I wrote, he curled up on the floor by the bunk in the aft cabin and did not disturb me. When we played, his eyes never left my face. When I was sad, he would lie in bed and press his little black nose against my cheek and stare calm and goodness into my eyes. He would sometimes nest in a pile of ropes waiting for me to come up on deck, and move his paws across the deck now and then to sniff his patience through the hatch over my cabin.

On Thanksgiving Day, 1990, we married. He was on sabbatical and I did not enroll in college that semester. We had just arrived in the Bahamas with *Sarabande* when I turned twenty-one years old. Although I was not expecting him, Father flew in from Puerto Rico. When I told him on the phone that I was getting married, he said, "But are you crazy?" It didn't matter that I'd been living with this man for over two years. I had refused to go back home time and time again. When we spoke I was always told I was loved and missed. I lived with a former professor of mine whom I was in love with, but in my father's eyes I seemed to behave as if I was simply hanging around overseas en route to graduate school. It was not Father's fault entirely. It was the nature of our relationship, an apparently silent, unconditional one of mixed messages that had plagued our lives: I love you enough to not care to ask important questions that will complicate things.

At the civil ceremony, my father stood between Alba and me on the balcony of a rented house facing the sea of Abaco and my husband's sailboat. The setting sunlight gave my father's features a slack, melting quality that was not far from expressing despair. At one point, when he took his ring off to lend it to the man I was marrying because he had not bothered to buy one and would never wear one, my father looked at me with such emotion, such regret mixed with longing and worry, that I lost my breath. Afterward, toasting straight from the rum bottle he carried, I overheard my father joking with my husband while pointing toward me, "Being young doesn't stink as much when you are a married woman." He was right.

In the morning, my father handed me back the partial manuscript of the memoir I'd been working on and shared with him. I had been awake most of the night, fearful of what he would feel, think, say, when he saw his portrait, the obvious connections between his actions and my mother's unhappiness and ultimate death. I had tried to be impartial, nonjudgmental, in the writing of it, but there was little I could do to offset the script of the loving yet sinister drama of their lives, the backdrop of my childhood. Ashamed, I looked into his eyes intent on assuring him that if there was anything he disagreed with I would not publish the book.

"Honesty, Irene, is the only thing we can hold on to and know it won't let us down," he said, shaking his head and staring down at the manuscript on my lap. "That is some book. I'm proud."

Later, I wished I'd had the words to strike up a conversation, to talk about the aspects of my origins that still baffled me, in spite of the words strewn together in a book. As it was, nothing else was said then or later. I gave him a hug and he slapped my butt. It was time for breakfast. But I could not eat from the nausea of a sixth pregnancy.

. . .

Back in Syracuse, Oliveira waited in the snow-covered car while I picked up a Western Union transfer from my dad. Money in hand, we drove to an abortion clinic in Rochester, New York. As with Dr. N, I was ashamed to go back to Dr. Y. We parked under a tree. The abandoned nest of a squirrel hung low by the passenger-side window. Pieces of newspaper were woven into the gray, cotton-like webbing of the nest. Inside the clinic, in the recovery room, I was given three Oreo cookies. Back in the car Oliveira sniffed his patience through the half-open window. When I gave him the cookies he ignored them and licked my neck instead. Oliveira had become the expression of my hope.

The fall after our wedding, in 1991, I submitted a partial manuscript of the memoir to an editor I had read about in a *New York Times* interview. I had gone to the college bookstore, bought *Writer's Market*, and found his address in New York. One day in early November right after terminating my seventh pregnancy, I stopped at the university post office to mail the package to the editor. By summertime in 1992, I had an agent, a publishing contract, and an advance payment. My husband marveled at my bold move, applauded my work ethic, and encouraged me, though I knew he could not come to terms with how the "homework" he had given me to stay busy while he wrote had turned into an actual book. As for me, a sense of validation anchored me to a writing life I had once adopted artificially. My days took on an independent quality, a relevance and direction of my own making. He seemed to make sense of my achievement by taking credit for it. When the subject of the sale of the book came up at social gatherings—he always made sure it would—I said it was all because of him.

Since my first pregnancy in 1987 I had had, on average, an abortion every eight months. Now, from the time I reached out to an editor and got a contract for a book, it would be eighteen months before I got pregnant again, for the eighth time, in July 1993. The only other significant stretch of time like this one would be the sixteen months following the publication of the book in August 1996. I don't think these symmetries were a coincidence. In these heightened moments of creativity and validation, I evaded the drama of pregnancy and abortion and "remembered" to take my birth control pills.

Each January, beginning in 1992, we drove to Florida and took a cargo ship to Man-O-War Cay in the Bahamas for a seven-month stay aboard *Sarabande*. He taught half the year and earned half a salary. Seasons went by quietly, interrupted or sewn together by an intermittent financial crisis—it was difficult to maintain a boat on half a salary.

Throughout the years living aboard *Sarabande*, I woke at dawn, got Oliveira in the dinghy and took him for a walk at the nearest beach. On my return, by 7:00 AM or so, I cooked breakfast, made coffee, baked bread, got lunch going on the stove, swept the floorboards, disinfected the head, went up on deck with the dog and put the sun cover on to cool off the boat through the day. Then I spent some time rinsing off the decks with buckets of salt water, polishing the winches, tending the teak, bailing the dinghy, conditioning its rubber, treating its aluminum floors against corrosion. I was usually done in time to serve him lunch during a writing break. In the afternoons I read or wrote in between dives overboard. Late in the afternoon he would emerge from the main cabin with pages for me to read.

By 4:00 PM or so we would get in the dinghy and go to a secluded cove where he would swim while I walked the dog again. Back on board he took a shower down below and I one up on deck. I made dinner while he sat in the cockpit watching boats come into the harbor and anchor. Over dinner it was my turn to discuss what I had worked on that afternoon. He listened attentively if what I had to say seemed interesting, but grew bored, and literally dozed off, if it did not.

Needless to say, many times dinner sent him right off to bed. I then stayed behind in the cockpit dreaming up better selves. I breathed in the evening and followed the course of the stars. There was hope in the air. Boats came in and went out on circumnavigations. I lived their stories, felt their excitement, and dreamt up my own rounding of Cape Horn. A minimalist spirit guided my days. I did not desire anything more than to resume the task at hand, the tending of a boat, a man, a dog, a book.

In June 1993 I received the first translated chapters of the memoir in the mail. The translation—and the passage of time since I had first written the book—revealed substantial fissures in the story. I had to ask myself new questions that opened up new problems, especially around my grandmother's life in New York City and my mother's past suicide attempts. My ideas for how to tackle them differed from what he thought should be done. The editing process created a new tension between us that sometimes felt competitive and other times patronizing. Our disagreements began to grow more frequent, branching out from writing and into daily life.

During our summers in Man-O-War Cay, my father would visit on infrequent weekend trips and my sisters would come stay for weeks at a time. When my father arrived on the island that July with his brother, Tío Miguel, my brother Cheo, and my two sisters, my husband acted like a trapped beast. Though my relatives had rented a house for the four days they were there, he complained about the lack of freedom and the interruption of his schedule. Each time we returned to the boat from a meal with my family he had to magnify their tics and antics: my father's inability to ask questions and his backward interest in cars, cockfighting, dominoes and horses; my brother's submissive relationship to my father and his limited intellect and obsession with food and women; Tío Miguel's Episcopalian Priesthood that clashed with his secular Judaism; my sisters' "neurotic" attachment to me. He always summed it up with the all too familiar proclamation that families were nests of suffering and civil war and a threat to love. Having my sisters over for another month-long stay with us on the boat was just too much for him. Why did I need that escape, right when I was supposed to be editing the translation of my book?

I didn't know what to say. I was the happiest hugging them to sleep, feeding them a vegetarian diet they hated but learned to love, and watching them learn how to trim a sail, jump off the boat into the bay, and read the night sky. Yet, when I pressed my body against his in bed, I feared losing his love. I felt cornered, obliged to choose between him and my life.

In July I was pregnant, for the eighth time. In January again, for the ninth time. Our relationship was strained, the edits on my book were coming to an end, and I returned to irregular birth control. He told me I had to be angry with him to keep on doing this. He called it "a narcissistic wound." He thought writing was not helping. I believed him.

Between the eighth and ninth abortions, I swallowed the contents of a bottle of painkillers a doctor had prescribed for the migraine-like headaches I'd been having. I followed the pills with a full eight-ounce glass of vodka. When I woke up my husband and Mercedes were standing on each side of me at the hospital. I had a tube in my mouth. My stomach was being pumped. Tears ran down the side of his nose while the most loving eyes I had ever seen on him looked down at me.

Not long after the final, edited translation was sent to the editor in 1994, I turned almost passionately to a novel I had begun two years earlier. I could sense he disliked my dedication, but he soon got to thinking the new book could bring us an advance contract and money to buy us a new boat engine. His initial hesitation turned to pressure overnight. I had to write a proposal and a sample. I had to learn how to write fiction. I had to listen to him and correct my writing along the lines of his editorial advice. My characters were hollow and romantic, and the premise of my story—the relationship between my grandmother and a Puerto Rican nationalist—was cliché. But he would protect me from ridicule.

One day I shocked myself by hating his ideas and edits. When I asked him to let me be, I could not believe my words. Soon I even began to dislike his writing. In the summer of 1994, when he turned sixty, I saw he was becoming frail. Our relationship would not recover from this knowledge.

Hurricane Chris began as a patch of thunderstorm over western Africa. It moved out over the Atlantic as a rainy, low-pressure wave. By Monday, August 17, the ham radio weather broadcast announced that it had intensified into a tropical storm. By Wednesday the 19th, pushed westward by a high-pressure zone to the north, the storm built strength over open ocean. The predicted course put the hurricane over the northeastern Bahamas within three days. He said we had to leave immediately and beat the storm. *Sarabande* had to be safely tied up in a canal in Ft. Lauderdale. We would lose her if we let her ride out the hurricane in the Bahamas.

By 1994, I could speak my mind here and there. Having written a book had given me some status. I said the bay we were moored in was a hurricane hole, after all. It probably made more sense to stay. There were mangroves all around to let us tie multiple lines to shore and cushion the boat if she broke loose. The ham radio weatherman, famous for accurate predictions, had assured listeners that the storm would intensify.

He sat at the captain's desk while I spoke, looking at several books on heavy-weather sailing spread open before him. I wasn't sure he was listening to me. I walked over and put my cheek on his shoulder. I said it was safer to stay. What if the boat broke down on the nonstop, twenty-eight-hour trip to the States? What if we hit coral on the banks at night? We had never crossed the banks at night in five years of cruising the Bahamas.

He looked up and said there could only be one captain on a boat. I was to get the boat ready. We were leaving in an hour. I was reassured by his forceful manner. He must know what he was doing, I thought.

Five hours later the injectors clogged and the engine seized. We headed slowly under sail, in almost no wind, to a nearby Cay. Shortly before dropping the anchor, I was able to bleed the engine but our alternator was not charging. We had to stay overnight and get it fixed the next day, if possible.

In the morning the ham radio announced that the storm had gained speed and was moving at twelve miles per hour. We had been able to buy a rebuilt alternator from a fellow cruiser, but the island's mechanic was in Florida on a doctor's visit. We could not find anyone to do the job.

Over lunch I saw concern for the first time in his disorganized, hesitant movements around the cabin. I asked what we should do. He said we would have to set out all our anchors and let the boat ride out the storm.

"What about us?"

"We'll find shelter on the island," he said. "If not, we will just have to ride it out on board. It was your original idea, wasn't it?"

For the first time, I sensed he had lost control. The knowledge was disconcerting, but it sent me into a militant, maternal mode to save him from the defacement I was witnessing. I said I was going to install the alternator myself and that we would be on our way by nightfall. Something in my voice or demeanor must have held utter persuasion because when I asked for the engine manuals, he handed them to me without a word of protest or sarcasm, and, to my shock, with trust in his eyes.

Early in the morning the next day, we were entering the Gulf Stream. We had sailed under power over the banks some ninety miles through the night and not hit ground or coral. I had steered most of the way with both radar and GPS helping me decipher the treacherous currents. Dead reckoning at night in the banks with a seven-and-a-half-draft sailboat was dangerous, if not impossible. When the sun finally came up and I saw the indigo blue of the stream against the white hull of *Sarabande* and the entrance landmark of Memory Rock behind me, I let go of my tight grip on the steering wheel, finally, and was sent to tears.

I turned off the engine and stared at the sails, flapping in the light wind. He was asleep below. He had relinquished all navigation, charting, and judgment to me. As much as I told myself that he had simply put me to the test, I knew that he had not had a choice. I completed what remained of the crossing, secured the boat in a deep canal far inland from the Fort Lauderdale harbor, and rushed back up to New York in quiet, chilling panic.

On Friday, September 24, 1994, my brother Miguel's body was found in the gutter behind a housing project in Puerto Rico. My stepmother called me around five in the afternoon: "They found Miguel."

The last time I had seen him, he was standing at a bus stop, barefoot, a small paper bag clenched in his hands. It was the second day of a short visit to Puerto Rico in 1991. I went down for three days to interview my two uncles for my book, along with three of my mother's best friends and my father. I was at my brother Cheo's house sipping coffee when the phone rang. Miguel, who'd been missing for weeks and had a warrant out for breaking his parole, was on the other end. I heard him say "Irene!" with genuine excitement, and immediately afterward, he said he was hungry and needed money to catch the bus back to the rehab center.

Cheo and I were stuck in a traffic jam half a block from where Miguel was waiting. I could see him sitting on a low cement wall, folding and unfolding a paper bag, his legs shaking. I finally opened the window and called out to him. Inside the car he couldn't stop shaking. When I asked what was wrong, his eyes filled with tears.

He told me to forgive him. It was simply impossible to change his life. He had tried but there was no use. There was no filthier trash in the world than he. He didn't want anyone to see him. He just wanted ten dollars to get himself across the island. What about the damned traffic jam? Nothing was moving. He was a whore. How was Dad doing? Miguel worried about his drinking. Had I moved back to the island? He really only needed ten dollars and he would be on his way. He didn't want to be a problem.

Shocked at the sight of my brother, the state of his arms, the missing front tooth, the black and blue marks covering his neck, the stained pants and torn shirt, the fact that he was only twenty-nine but looked like he was forty, I couldn't find a better thing to say but ask about his shoes. Cheo signaled me in the rearview mirror to shut up. Miguel opened the door to leave and from the back seat I reached out and pulled him back. I told him he could change. He had to make an effort. What the hell was wrong with him anyway? He turned, despair in his eyes that frightened me, and said, "I'm sorry. I just need those ten dollars."

I pulled out a twenty from my purse and handed it to him, and before I could say a thing he was out and lost between the cars. He left the paper bag behind. Inside there was a yellow toothbrush.

Cheo shrugged his shoulders. "Forget it. He'll be back."

He was teaching his evening seminar. I called the airlines, made reservations, and packed for the two of us. I sat in the only chair in the living room, waiting.

Why hadn't I done more for Miguel? Why did I ignore his phone calls? Even if he was calling to ask for money or a plane ticket, I should have at least given him the cushion of my sisterly presence. I could have told him a hundred times how much I loved him, how much I wished he wasn't suffering, how much I wanted to help. I didn't have to plead with my husband to lend me some money to send to my brother. I didn't have to put up with his long speeches about how families are always a big problem and how they are the biggest threat civilization devised against desire. I only needed to remind my brother he was loved.

Miguel was a heroin addict. He cheated and lied and stole from friends and relatives, yet he was the tenderest person I had ever met. He never stole from strangers. Each time an uncle or aunt complained about a missing VCR or TV or radio, I thought, way to go Miguel, as long as you turn to us instead of the neighbors, I know there is hope.

Sitting on that chair, despairing over my brother's death, I began to grow bitter at my husband and at myself. A few times I went to the kitchen and poured myself a shot of his whisky. I went back again to that chair in the middle of an empty room, as if to a defendant's bench, pushed by a need to find all the evidence I could against the life I was leading. I looked around me and wished I could have a home with furniture like normal people, a bed off the floor, a bookshelf that wasn't a filing box. He refused to buy things for the apartment because they tied him down. He wanted to have a light load for all the moves he put us through each semester we came back from the boat. He rented only one semester a year to save on the other months of rent when we were away.

The bitterness mounted and I began to feel angry. Why is this happening to me? I asked in frustration. Why did my brother have to die? Why am I pregnant again? What the hell am I going to do this time? I fell asleep on the chair with my feet propped up on the suitcase.

When I woke to the sound of the keys in the door, I knew I was not in love with my husband any longer. I told him about Miguel. He hugged me for a long time without saying a word. Finally, growing restless in his embrace, I looked up at him.

I had to understand his problem with airplanes. He just couldn't do it. His tone was soft and caring. When I reminded him of the martinis he had on his way to Amsterdam for the shows he curated and how he had fared well, his tone became severe. Families, I had to remember, are dangerous. To finally meet my extended family under these circumstances would not be a good thing for our relationship. Funerals, weddings, graduations, birthdays, all these family gatherings were a breeding ground for relatives to tear at the walls of one's private and inner world.

Our age difference would surely be a perfect blank canvas for anybody's displacement of pain. He had to protect us from that. I would be okay, he told me. I was a strong person now, after all these years. He had taught me how to look through acts and words for danger. He trusted I was going to be just fine by myself. As he said this, I realized I was actually quite content to go alone, after all.

My childhood friend Maria picked me up at the airport. I didn't want my father or any other relative to come get me. I asked her to take me to her apartment first. There I drank a few shots of rum, took a double dose of my migraine medication, and finally cried.

The funeral home wasn't sign-posted and we lost our way in the town where I grew up before we found the low, concrete building on a corner off Main Street. Inside, relatives sat on chairs lined against the wall. No one except my father, Cheo, Uncle Miguel, and my sisters had seen me since 1987. Hugs were followed by remarks on my absence, hair, weight, the white outfit I'd chosen to wear. I wanted to see my brother once more. Miguel was lying in a small, bare room lined with more chairs where people sat whispering in low voices. His head was thrown back, his arms stretched out along the sides of the mauve lining of the coffin.

The burial took place the following Tuesday. In the cemetery, I saw what remained of my oldest brother, Fonso. Addicted to heroin and crack, his six-foot-four, emaciated frame barely sustained him. Thin and feeble, little was left of him. He had lost his job, his wife, his children, and his dignity. His younger brother had just died, overdosed and beaten to death while in search of yet another fix. Fonso followed my father everywhere with a pained look. It was the family gossip that my father had resorted to giving Fonso money for drugs in the last months since Miguel disappeared. He wanted to protect Fonso from the horror of withdrawal that had sent Miguel into the streets willing to do anything for a last fix. Like with Miguel, no program, no jail term or court-ordered rehab program had done a thing for Fonso. Father seemed to have learned from Miguel that you feed your son, you don't let him prostitute himself, and you wait to see if a miracle happens. As my father's mother always said: "Nobody is dead until they are dead." A wave of respect for my father's loving care came over me as I saw him standing beside his two brothers officiating at the service, the shadow of his oldest son shaking behind him.

There they both were, the two Episcopalian Vilar priests, my father's brothers, conducting the funeral just as seventeen years earlier they had stood together blessing the marriage of my brother Cheo and days later my mother's funeral. It was too much to bear. I was about to walk back to the car when it became clear that nobody was stepping forward to speak on Miguel's behalf. My father was rooted to the floor. Cheo was last seen bent over a bush sobbing like a child. Fonso stood hunched over, his arms wrapped tightly around his own chest. A righteous combativeness came over me. I walked up to my uncles and said I would speak for my brother. All around me, eyes sighed in relief. As I spoke, I had the piercing recognition we were all stuck together in the same picture, trapped forever in a drama with seemingly no end. Afterward, Miguelito's body was lowered on top of my mother's. When the lid of the grave shut, I felt mother and son had broken free. I walked up to Fonso. His eyes lit up on calling me "Dumbo," my childhood nickname. He was wearing a satin-like, long-sleeved red shirt. I hugged him and was caught in the sweat and stench of a chest I couldn't seem to get a grasp around. Afterward, people gathered at my aunt's house. My family thought it was a good thing Miguel had died. Now he rested in peace, they said. I couldn't understand. I flew back to Syracuse in the morning.

The days after I arrived, all I did were the daily chores necessary to keep things going: cooking, making the bed, walking the dog, photocopying my husband's materials for class, brewing his coffee. Quite often I forgot what I was doing and found myself wandering from room to room. To read or to write was impossible. The worst moments were when I left home and went to his office on campus. I would be walking down the halls of his department and suddenly it would hit me: "Miguel will never be alive again." I would go to the bathroom and wash my hands trying to not look into the mirror. A few times I caught a glimpse of myself and it would hit me again: "You didn't help him."

I felt emptier and lighter, like a bubble. Each morning I tried to work on the novel, but by nighttime I grew silent and disoriented.

One day my husband stood by my bedside and said my moods would end up killing our love story. He said it was my brother's funeral, my mother's suicide, a biography weighing on me. I looked at him suspiciously and answered in my head. I had the words to speak but I wasn't sure he deserved my anger. For seven years he had taught me plenty of words but somewhere along the way I had learned to distrust most of what came out of my mouth.

Our quarrels grew increasingly turbulent. The veins on my forehead often swelled. His mouth trembled as we raised our voices.

"What's happening to us? We never said such terrible things to each other," I said.

"This is the end of a love story, that's what's happening."

"Are you sure?"

"Oh, yes," he said with a mocking smile. "One always kills what one loves."

I was no longer the pliant college teenager he had met one fall semester in his class on the writer Juan Rulfo. I was bitter and impatient and at twenty-five, approaching thirty. He always thought he knew me. It wasn't his fault really. I led him to believe he could know me.

It was December, more than three months since we'd moved in for the new semester, and most of the moving boxes remained unopened. It was the same story each fall and winter. In December, I packed up our things and put them in storage in different friends' basements. The reverse applied when we arrived in September. I usually packed or unpacked at night, while he slept, using the prospect of seeing his relieved face when he woke up as motivation for completing the boring task.

But this time I felt annoyed when I began to unpack. I was upset at feeling this way. I attributed it to exhaustion from the trip back to Syracuse after being chased by a hurricane, and then Miguel's death and the anxiety of the novel waiting on my desk. I was dreading conflicts with him when I worked on it. Disagreeing with his suggestions often led to accusations that writing was going to my head and to suppers eaten in silence.

The pages he wrote for his own book seemed increasingly flawed when they'd once been perfect. I didn't like seeing this. He also had to undo people's lives, find a weakness to chew on. Once in a while he would turn to me and ask if I had noticed this or that. I would say yes, of course. Although his constant insights into my behavior had once kept me from breaking a glass or bumping into things, when I did act clumsily and he warned me against my unconscious, it now sounded old.

More than anything else, what alarmed me was that he had a body odor now and I was repelled. I too had a body odor. I attributed it to pregnancy and began to reject it. For the first time in all the pregnancies, I was unable to imagine myself a mother. I would lie in the bathtub, trying to project our threesome of a family into the future. When I couldn't, I had to leave the bathroom and pour myself a drink. One day I poured myself a few drinks before the bath and tried again. But instead of a family, I surprised myself by seeing James staring into my eyes and I felt my body quiver with desire. It had been four years. We picked up where we had left off; at the university hotel bar I had last seen him drunk. I asked him to meet me there that same night. I was pregnant for the tenth time.

During the two-month-long renewed affair I wore heavy makeup for the first time, and felt more cheerful. I stayed in the apartment more often rather than go to my husband's office, did not complain when he had to stay late at work or when he had to go to Manhattan for a business meeting. Instead, I said I would work on the book. Ever since he met me, I had bought my clothes at the Salvation Army, but now, out of the blue, I ordered a small wardrobe from a clothes catalogue. Not that he minded. I had a right to use my writing money in whatever way I pleased, but he found it suspicious. I had even suggested staying in Syracuse for the spring term so I could finish the novel instead of going to the boat. I could do the work on the boat, he said. Didn't I write the damned first book on the boat to begin with? I was amazed at his observations, almost flattered.

Then, one Sunday afternoon he saw me come out of James's apartment building when I was supposed to be at the library. We all lived in the same complex and he confronted me in the parking lot. I did not respond and he hit the hood of his car with his fist. It made a light dent. I saw anger and humiliation distorting his face, his voice breaking as he almost begged me to tell him. I had to and as I did, I thought of Mercedes. I saw him get in the car in a fury, yelling how could I do this to him, and with that man, that pathetic Mormon of a teacher who couldn't write.

A few hours later, he called and asked me to meet him at a restaurant. When I arrived, I saw a man uneasy in his chair, impatient with the waitress, annoyingly turning a spoon in his hand. It was not until the wine was poured into our glasses that he said anything. He took a big gulp, fastened his tired, dark-green eyes on me, and asked if I was in love with James Merton. I was moved, relieved that the attack I expected wasn't happening. I told him the truth. I wasn't.

I was about to reassure him of my love when he interrupted me and said it was all Mercedes's fault. He had been afraid of something like this happening since our friendship began. She was living vicariously through me. And I, I was depressed and acting out, needing to escape facing my demons, mainly my mother. What better way than an old professor who preyed on students and who probably appealed to my narcissism by saying how great I was? He understood. We had to get away from these pathetic characters, like Mercedes and James. We needed to get to *Sarabande.* Things like this didn't happen on a boat for a reason. A boat kept one honest.

An anger I had never felt came over me, and a desire to hurt him. I said I was not sure of my feelings for him. I needed time. I was not going to the boat anytime soon. I panicked hearing myself, and as I stood up to leave, I said I loved him. He left for New York City that same evening.

In the morning I walked to James's apartment telling myself I could love him, hopeful that with time I could grow used to him.

I was almost happy, even excited, about this new systematic thinking on relationships. When I knocked at the door, I could smell James's pipe and the coffee machine brewing. I didn't wait and used the key he'd given me to let myself in. He was sitting on the sofa in his pajamas holding Mia, the graduate student, in his arms. She was naked. On the end table were two empty bottles of wine. I ran down the stairs in a panic knowing I was now a willing prisoner of my master.

In the evening I was not feeling well from nausea and Mercedes came by. I sat in a corner of the living room sipping tea and chewing on a lemon while she looked through a photo album that traced seven years between me and him and a number of pictures showing my friendship with Alba. As I refilled her teacup, I noticed tears in her eyes. I asked what was wrong. She asked if I was happy. I said of course I was. She asked why I thought I kept getting pregnant. I was not good with pills, I answered. I just couldn't remember to take them. She was about to speak, but changed her mind. She nodded her head as if she understood and sent me for an ashtray.

Mercedes accompanied me to my gynecologist's office the next day. Dr. Y had carried out close to half of all the abortions (four out of nine). He took me to his office and sat me down in front of a stack of newspapers. His picture stared up at me from a page of the *Syracuse Herald*. In 1994 his clinic had been attacked with butyric acid. He pointed at the stack and said he risked his life every day by coming to his office and supporting a women's right to choose. But I was not choosing, was I?

This abortion would be the fifth I asked him to perform in six years. It was hard for him to think of the lives he put on the line, his and his family's, in the name of women who did not care.

"I care," I said, on the brink of tears, "I just keep forgetting to take my pill."

"Then you need to consider other methods of birth control." His voice softened a bit. "Or better perhaps, your husband needs to consider them. Have him come in and we can discuss the options together."

Before the procedure, Dr. Y explained that my cervix seemed inflamed. This tenth termination was particularly painful. He recommended a couple of tests for when I returned. As he was leaving the room, I thanked him. "There is nothing to thank me for," he said, placing his hand on my head. "Just take care of yourself."

And so from January 1995 to August 1995, I was responsible for an affair, a suicide attempt, three car accidents, two boat collisions, and two abortions. My weight dropped to ninety-five pounds and I had trouble sleeping. I lost my temper and felt like crying at the slightest provocation. Other times, I hid myself in the bathroom, my heart racing, wanting to push everything away. I felt I was going mad. Yet, we hung in there as a couple, my husband and I, revitalized in part by my pathetic drama. He took it on himself to "save" me. Two more years would go by before I could stand the discovery that my master did not exist.

A lba was working on her doctorate at Cornell and seldom came back to visit, but Mercedes and I would spend the evenings he taught his seminars together, roaring with laughter. Mercedes. Her face often appears before me at night when I close my eyes. The face is usually followed by images of a dinner that never took place, with Alba, Rosa, Aileen, Janet, Kelly, Anne, Gina, Veronique, Ursula, Eva, Lissette, Joan, and Mercedes sitting at the table. I gather them to say how much they all mean to me, how I can't think of my struggle with depression without each of them pointing out a way of being that was dignified and courageous. I am pouring wine into their glasses, watching them eat with pleasure, hearing them laugh, and once in a while look up at me with love.

Important events in my life, like that dinner, have not happened except in my mind. I love my father, and as much as I've told myself to call him on his birthday, I never have. This call, however, thrives in my memory with more presence and resonance than the love itself and the things that indeed have taken place. I wonder if it was the same with Mercedes.

From the moment I met her in 1985, I was attracted by her contempt for life in America, her sharp sarcasm, her pointed sincerity, her anger at not having lived the many lives she could have had if not for her husband's profession. She did not smile easily. She smiled only when she felt like it, never out of politeness, like other people, like myself. She also kept her distance from things. Impassive to the world, indifferent to God—she was now a self-proclaimed atheist—critical of everything human, she sat on her couch in the living room of a Victorian home, chain smoking and taking nothing seriously except people's absurd behaviors and her husband's when he brought her to America for a year and stayed for twenty.

Her life, I would find out, was a prison in which she smoked to keep busy and forget. With an unforgiving and talented eye, she edited her husband's poetry books and read avidly every day. But besides these two activities, she seemed to wait—for what, I didn't know. I'm not sure she knew. She sat on that brown couch most of the day, fastening her eyes and ears on whoever sat across from her, her husband's colleagues or his graduate students, speaking of deconstruction and the mistakes of Freud, while waiting. She spoke from the sublime height of a hermit in his retreat, as if acquainted with some secret that was hidden to others but revealed to her. In a way, she shared a lot of my husband's intellect and mannerisms, but from the Victorian trenches of her living room, there wasn't much harm she could do. And she was a mother.

She was a mother and a wife and did not shy away from these choices, did not speak of freedom at the expense of the values around which she had built her life. I found her simply striking, a presence impossible to shake off, a fearless woman. She did not wish to change the life that imprisoned her.

Sometime in late 1994, sitting on the shores of Cazenovia Lake, discussing the author Bachelard and my memoir, I had told Mercedes I had written about my mother's death as my redemption instead of my doom. She widened her eyes, sucked in her cheeks, and then opened her mouth slightly while her tongue pushed against her left cheek, something she did when she thought hard about anything that bothered her. Finally, she took a cigarette to her mouth and inhaled long and deep.

"Your ideas are fashionable," she said after some time, "but you don't know what you are talking about." She pinched my ear, her eyes lit up with a smile.

"You're a dear child, even though you can be tiresome at times. Beware of other people's ideas. They are wrong most of the time. You'll come to your own soon enough. You'll see."

Sometimes her honesty could be as crushing as my husband's, but with her I never felt shame. I was fascinated by her direct, pointed ways, attracted by the discovery that a woman could be that unswerving, unyielding, almost cruel. She did not care if you loved, liked, approved of her.

Watching Mercedes argue with my husband was nerve-racking. I usually excused myself and found something to do in the kitchen while they went at it at the dining table or in the living room. They had known each other for the greater part of twenty years. He had met Mercedes as a young woman, witnessed the course of her bitterness toward the world, and said a toast on her fiftieth birthday. There was a shared past and a shared nostalgia for their countries of origin, and of course, they'd read the same books, asked themselves the same existential questions, and resigned themselves to the same unmemorable Syracuse.

What truly set them apart were Mercedes's hatred for authoritarian figures, her suspicion toward men and women in general, and his narcissism. Mercedes never nurtured his ego and he, I would come to understand, couldn't take that. One day he called her the most intelligent woman he'd ever met, the next day, a man hater.

One evening, over dinner at her house, he stood up from the table and threw his napkin on the plate, saying to Mercedes that the problem between them was that he was still a romantic, a child inside, unafraid to allow for the mystery of experience—after all, his doctorate was in religion—while she was a reductionist, spoiled by the Spanish communist party she once pledged alliance to, by the authoritarian ways of the Franco times she had grown up in, and by the absurd French feminists she read. He headed for the door and signaled me to follow.

I hesitated. I looked at Mercedes, pleading. She winked back, assuring me it was okay. I should go. Her friendship would always be there, waiting. I left with an overwhelming desire to stay behind with her, listening to the marvelous and funny ways she could spin out her miseries. I don't think anyone has ever made me laugh as much and hard as she did.

When summer 1995 came around, we were still in Syracuse and I was pregnant again. I didn't tell him this time. He was wrapping up the writing for an art exhibit catalog. When the day of our departure to the boat neared I made up all kinds of excuses not to go to *Sarabande*. The truth was I wasn't ready to go away. I didn't know why exactly, but Mercedes and the pregnancy were part of the reason. She had told me only the month before that she had kidney cancer. She had known for a while but had not made up her mind what to do. It was a dangerous Stage III cancer and the kidney had to come out. She needed to undergo chemotherapy. I asked how long she waited to start treatment. I finally understood the tears of that evening when she asked me why I kept on getting pregnant. Facing death, life had turned less absurd.

As for me, I was increasingly numb. Every time he had sex with me I went to tap trees in the woods of New Hampshire. I was ten years old and back in Boynton School. One day he threatened to leave alone for the boat if I didn't join him. I wasn't sure what I felt. He finally went to New York. It was the day after Mercedes's surgery.

A week later Mercedes came home from the hospital. Alba and I sat at her bedside and watched her sleep. At one point she opened her eyes and smiled weakly. She wanted a cigarette. When we reminded her that cigarettes were the cause of her illness, her expression turned severe. She asked us to leave. A minute later, we heard her scream. She was lying on the floor in the middle of the room, her long scar exposed under the robe, a pack of cigarettes in her hand.

As we carried her back to bed, she told us she was not going to have chemotherapy; she wanted to die with her hair in place and a cigarette in her mouth. Alba laughed a nervous laugh, telling her mother to get a good rest, that the day would come soon enough when she could have a smoke again. I burst into tears and ran out of the room to the phone. I needed him to come back and get me. I wanted to rush to the boat, away from everything and everyone, and resume our lives. It was all sudden and unexpected. The change perplexed me. I tried not to think about it. In the morning of the day we drove south, I was nauseous with an eleventh pregnancy I endured on the boat.

Most of the fall and spring of 1996 escapes me. I know I read several books a week. I know I "loved" him again. And I know that soon after my return to Syracuse, the days acquired an exciting, creative quality as the publication of the memoir drew near. I began to write again. I received in the mail a heavy box filled with Freedom of Information Act documents I fought hard for and finally got. With these files the novel became more real. I put my birth control pills right on top of the night table and I seldom skipped one. When my book was published the following summer I read from it at the local Barnes & Noble in front of three hundred people. I was not going to go mad. I was going to be okay. When the tension between my husband and me increased during the book tour and his mocking criticism of my commitment to help publicize the memoir gnawed at my confidence, I still felt I was going to be okay.

I saw little of Mercedes over this time, as my renewed pact with him demanded I cut out socializing during the four months we lived in Syracuse in the fall. Over that time, too, Mercedes went to Spain for a year when her sister committed suicide. In October 1997, we picked up where we had left off. After finding out I was pregnant for the twelfth time, I went straight to her house. She told me to keep the baby. I was twenty-eight years old. He was not going to leave me if I insisted on having the baby, not after all we'd been through. What was the matter with me? I still remember her stunned face when I told her I didn't want a child any longer. I was stunned myself.

In December 1997, he said, "We have to get out of here. Both the body and the brain grow crippled in these winters."

We sat at a table in the sun, looking out over the narrow main street of the college town. We were the only ones in the restaurant sitting out in the piercing cold.

"I know. There is nothing like warm weather," I said.

He looked at me suspiciously. I was sucking on a lemon.

"The boat is the only solution. Sailing. The ocean is the last frontier," he announced as if for the first time. "If we left for the boat right now and forgot all about your paperback release and your interviews, we would surely rejuvenate. Wouldn't you want that?"

Was he punishing me for my swift agreement with him a moment earlier? He knew I had no desire to go to the boat. He was doing it again. He had provoked the argument he wanted.

"Why do you ask me if I want to go to the boat when you know as well as I do that I can't?"

I sensed the aggression brewing, the way he half closed his eyes.

"Well," he said. "You've truly become like any other woman at twenty-eight, bitter and afraid of turning thirty. You've done so faster than I predicted, though."

It was true. I had changed.

"Do you think it's wise to abandon what you worked so hard at?" I asked.

"What?"

"The book. The book that's gone to my head and that you feel you wrote. What about the readings?"

I was pronouncing the words slowly.

"Maybe," I went on, "maybe it is wise after all . . ."

"Now, that's interesting! You're angry with me, aren't you? Isn't this the whole thing? Of course, Pygmalion all over again. Every single woman in my life hits twenty-eight and walks headfirst into a Pygmalion complex!" He got up from his chair and put his hands deep in his pockets.

There was something sad in his voice, even in his attack, and I had to remind myself that I wanted to remain angry rather than heartbroken about what was happening to us.

"You, Irene, you must do what you want to do instead of blaming me for not having the guts. And the book business, well, I should have known better, not even you are safe from a weak ego."

I felt the bitterness of his words, but I was not offended by his irony because I agreed with him.

"What I really want . . . well, I want you to let me write the book I want."

I spoke with a violence too new to let me speak without shaking.

"What on earth!" He shook his head as if he had run into a maze. "Is that it? You're so hung up with writing, but don't you see that it's all a big lie, you're falling for something that should never be taken seriously? I warned you, Irene. I knew it!"

"I just want to write the book I want to write without you reading and editing over my shoulder to save me from ridicule!"

He smiled.

"I won't wait for you. I've never waited for a woman in my life and I won't now.

"What irony," he went on, "what irony . . . I help you out, teach you all I know, and you resent me for it. To hell with you women."

He was right, no doubt, but how cold-hearted and stupid he was.

"I'm sorry," I said.

But he had already disappeared behind the building on the other side of the street.

On a train ride down to New York for the Christmas holidays of 1997, I told him I was pregnant again. He looked me in the eye with astonishment as if he had never been a part of the pregnancies or known about them. I was locked in repetition, compulsion, and an unstoppable desire to reenact, he said at the Erie Canal out the window. As always, he was right and he was wrong.

For him, the world was a trap in which we allowed ourselves to be ensnared. A childless life and sailing allowed him to avoid the world. But I had no other life to live but mine and I couldn't, didn't want to, avoid the world any longer.

When he was done talking, I too stared out at the Erie Canal, longing for the day when I would love someone again.

At a friend's house, I drank a glass of wine too many. The nausea from that pregnancy was the worst I had ever experienced. Sucking on a lemon had stopped helping, but I had discovered red wine took some of the edge off. I could go through a bottle on my own pretty fast. When I excused myself from the table for the evening, I saw his eyes reprimand me for leaving him alone. He disliked prolonged social contact and the more so without the buffer of my cheerful presence. Even the greatest friends bored him after half an hour. The best moments he spent with them happened when speaking of himself.

I went upstairs to our guest room certain I had made a fool of myself and I had let him down. The thought of his displeasure was unusually satisfying.

When he joined me not long after, he told me I had to stay away from wine if I didn't know how to drink like a lady. He then began getting ready for bed while putting down our hosts. Melissa, in her mid forties, was a talented artist, and her husband, Peter, thirty years her senior, was a famed physicist. There was an endearing tenderness between them and a peaceful companionship. I enjoyed being with them. To him, though, there was only boredom: Melissa's middle-aged fear, Peter's pending death, and a clumsy, big dog standing in for the child they didn't have.

We were in bed and could hear Peter clearing his throat in the bathroom next to our room while Melissa encouraged the dog to climb up to their bed. "You see what domesticity does," he said, too worked up for what the situation merited. "A dog becomes more interesting than his owners." Our own dog, Oliveira, was sleeping in the corner by the radiator.

It seemed to me that we ourselves were a version of our hosts. The only difference was that Melissa was a real woman, independent, secure, confident, and their relationship was respectful, mature, and one between equals. I sat up in bed and stared at Oliveira.

"What's wrong?" he asked. I was not following his deconstruction of others with interest and admiration. I would have preferred to be sleeping with my dog. When he asked again, "What's on your mind?" I lied.

"James," I said.

"Who's James?"

"Merton. James Merton."

He looked at me with condescending suspicion. I lied again:

"I'm just thinking how wrong things would have gone if I had chosen him above you."

He was clearly confused now and I felt a reckless excitement. *A ver, a ver . . .* "Let's see, let's see . . ." he said, or better "Go on, go on . . ." He sat up and brought his hands together in some solemn way that was all wrong.

I went on: "It's true that I didn't love him, but what Merton had to offer was definitely more tangible than what we have. I mean, here we are staying with friends you don't even respect for the lack of a better place, going back to Syracuse to an apartment I have to move us out of before the end of January . . ."

I couldn't make myself stop.

Then he asked the question I had waited over ten years to hear. Did I want a child? Maybe it was time for me to have a child, he said, turning on the light. He would do that if it were that important to me. I didn't have to have an abortion the next day. He wished it didn't have to happen this way, by accident, he wished I had made him part of the decision. In any event, he was ready to give me a child if that's what I wanted.

I was shocked. And I was even more shocked to realize I didn't want his child.

That night I kept thinking about James. At the back of my eyes, open to the darkness, impossible thoughts took shape: memories recapturing the happiness that James had made me feel.

At Washington Square, people were gathered in a circle between the fountain and the arch. A mime stared up at the sky, his body sliding sideways like a serpent. I turned onto Fifth Avenue and went to a café to meet with him. A few round, iron tables lined the sidewalk. He was seated out there, a cup to his mouth, looking at the passersby. He said he would stay there and read for a couple of hours. I made my way to the doctor's office wondering what I would be thinking on my way back. "It's nothing," as usual. "That was quick."

A nurse behind the front desk turned a page of *Parenting* magazine. Across the waiting room, a conversation between two young women had something to do with nose rings. I could tell which of them was there to end a pregnancy and which was the loyal friend. I began filling out the five color-coded forms.

The phone rang several times—people wanting an appointment or inquiring about opening hours. At one point, the receptionist said, "Go to Parkmed, and they'll tell you who can do it, no, no, we can't do it, you are too late." The person on the phone was bound to be more than twelve weeks pregnant. I was ten.

I stared at my blue piece of paper and looked for the one question that was not printed on the forms: You got yourself pregnant again?

The nurse called my name. In the small room, the doctor took my feet and placed them in padded stirrups. She asked if this was my first abortion. I heard myself lying: My first and my last.

The nurse held my hand and told me to relax. I stretched my left hand over my stomach in anticipation of the procedure and closed my eyes. The doctor called the attention of the nurse to the size of my uterus. It was orange sized rather than a lemon. I was closer to twelve weeks than to ten. At fourteen, she said, inserting the familiar cold, steel speculum, my uterus would feel like a grapefruit. Her voice was soft, almost tender, and did not stop for a second.

"This is the speculum . . . this is iodine soap . . . Now you may get a little rapid cramping over the next minute as I do the anesthetic injection . . . I'm going to open your cervix now . . . I only need to dilate to ten millimeters . . . Now there'll be some tugging and pulling . . . some cramping, not to worry."

There was a natural cadence to her words, a normalcy and a simplicity that clashed with my thoughts. I wanted nothing to distract from the anger at myself and at him sipping his coffee downstairs. I clenched my hand tightly on my vibrating stomach and swore that this time was absolutely the last. No more roaming the baby section at Marshall's whispering to a baby that was bound to not live. No more telling myself, "I will have you for a few months, then we'll see, at least I have you for a few months . . ." For too long I had been an ostrich that thinks it can elude the hunter by not looking at him.

"We are almost done, honey. You are tough as nails."

I walked out of the office in a trance. Once again I had been saved and damned at the same time. At the café, he had his legs stretched on the chair next to him, his head tilted back, his eyes closed.

Back in Syracuse, sometime in March, I had a dream about my childhood sweetheart, Abraham. I woke up with my heart aching in that old but recognizable way of feeling lovestruck. I walked around the house, made myself a bowl of cereal, and stared out the window at a snow-covered downtown Syracuse. I could not shake myself free from the spell. Frustrated that a dream could hold such power, I went back to bed intent on tossing and turning until he woke up. Having him back in the world of the living would blot it all out. Instead, he held me by the hips and tried to roll over on top of me.

I told myself he's your husband. I told myself all will pass soon enough. I told myself close your goddamn eyes and jump hop-scotch. But my body could only fight him and fly away from under him, and that's exactly what it did. Locked in the bath-room, I sat on the toilet, pregnant for the twelfth time and fallen out of love.

Early the next afternoon, I walked up the steps to James's office building and knocked at his door. We had not seen each other in three years, since the day I let myself in his apartment and found the naked Mia. He called many times then begging me to let him explain but I asked him to never call again. Now, I did not know what I was going to say. He welcomed me with a strong, long hug and stared goodness into my eyes. He got two copies of my book from the bookshelf and asked me to sign them; one to him, the other to his sister. We went to lunch. Walking to the Faculty Center restaurant, we crossed paths with my husband on his way to campus. He stopped, hands in the pockets, and shook his head all the while smiling contempt at us. I kept on walking. I turned once and saw him still standing in the same spot look-ing toward us.

I didn't feel anything for James but a deep appreciation for his appreciation of me. His manners were soothing, his voice quiet. James and I had nurtured a relationship in which I only wished to sit and talk with him. It was this way now more than ever. I clearly needed to leave my husband for good and had no idea how.

I didn't want to go home after lunch, but I did. I walked into our apartment feeling confident, but it didn't last long. He had it all figured out. He told me I had no guts to exit the relationship through the front door. Instead I had to jump out the window and break all the glass. He went on and on. All he said rang with truth, but now the truth didn't touch me, didn't seduce me. I began to pack. The more I packed, the angrier he became. I kept telling myself, say something, explain yourself, soothe his pain, but something had taken hold of me, a silence that grew the longer time passed. By the time I was at the door ready to leave, he took me by the arm and called me a whore.

I was thinking of a number of things to say, all dignified and proper, and yet the only thing I could do was smile. This final aggressive gesture took place almost simultaneously with the sharp crack of the slap that twisted my head violently toward the door. My eyes blurred with tears and I fixed my gaze on Oliveira, sitting by the bathroom door and staring at us. I didn't notice when he left. I was asking myself if I would ever be able to love again.

I moved to the apartment downstairs. I had no money, no furniture, no food, but a landlady's compassion gave me a set of keys to a furnished, one-bedroom unit on good faith. He waited, first angrily, then patiently, for me to return, but I never did. I called my father instead and told him I was on my own and needed help. He didn't ask me a question. He said he would send me money through Western Union, and to not rush into anything. Couples were bound to have these moments.

We carried out our divorce in the most unusual terms. Between April and June and over a couple of lunches, we filled out the divorce papers ourselves with no lawyer involved. I didn't want anything from him, alimony or payments of any kind. Awkwardly and ashamed I asked for a couple of thousand dollars to get me through a few months' rent until I found a job. He stipulated that a substantial lump-sum payment from his TIAA-CREF retirement come to me as a settlement. I was to keep three thousand dollars and use the rest to pay past due bills accrued in our relationship. A significant amount of money was needed to pay for the overdue mortgage on *Sarabande*. Between the new engine we put on the boat and charged to his American Express card, betting on the sale of my new book that didn't happen, and a lifestyle that never adjusted to his half a year salary, we were many thousands of dollars under. He held me responsible for half of it. We signed the papers and handed them to the court in July of 1998. Throughout these odd legalistic encounters with my husband, there was a strange, almost grotesque flirtatiousness cushioning the implosion of our relationship.

After many Western Union transfers and a couple of rent checks, my father and Cheo flew to Syracuse to help me move apartments. I was touched by the loving gesture and the realization that my family was there, always, if I cared to appreciate them for what they were. My father wanted me to go back to Puerto Rico for a while but I refused. I said I was looking into graduate school. He liked that. But I also grew impatient with his easy acceptance of everything. I had left my husband, and my father had not even asked me what had happened.

"If people divorce it's because they have to," he said. "The biggest things in life, like vocation and love and parenting, people have to come to in their own time and terms. If parents intrude it only makes things worse."

He was not comfortable speaking, but he went on: "I knew you two were not a good match. I had to wait and let things run their course. That's all a father can do, be there when he's needed."

At one point he asked one question: Was my ex-husband going to pay me any alimony after a decade together? When I explained the arrangement he chuckled.

Mercedes, though, was irate. When the settlement monies showed up in my account in October she had convinced me we should each keep half. How was I going to survive until my life got under way again? And hadn't most of my book advance gone to him and the boat anyway? She was right, though I was ashamed to need his money.

For the next several months, I daydreamed. In my daydreams I was making a new place my own, decorating, building and rebuilding a part of the room, the house, the apartment. I wasn't interested in why I was in a specific place, nor what had led me there. Independent of my personal history, the woman I imagined myself to be didn't have a past life, nor did she have relatives. She existed externally in the arrangement of the space she lived in, and living, always, was exemplified in sleeping and reading. These two spaces, the sleeping quarters and the living room, were central parts of the daydream. There were no kitchens.

I lived in an obsessive, thoughtless, decorating fantasy that kept me moving while my body grew slower, distancing from friends and relatives and staggering among the things and events of life like a sick person who finally gets up after being bedridden for months. I only felt normal when I was lying. It pleased me to get sick with a cold or a fever or a headache, since it seemed perfectly agreeable to my catatonic state. Outside, in the supermarket or the library, I would get dizzy, disoriented. Only in the dead air of a closed room could I breathe with some normalcy. I made my self a cloister and thrived in my smallness.

At times, mainly at mid-afternoon when the sun shone in a particularly merry way, I would open the living room window and look out on the bustle of campus life. Everything outside was alive under a blue sky and I would feel the hint of a desire to be different, out there, alive myself, but the sight of it all cut me like an indefinite pain, like a vague feeling of dissatisfaction, of a flawed life.

A few months after leaving my husband, I called Alba in Minnesota where she was teaching. She said she would fly in to see me the next day. Her alarm made me nervous. I reassured her, promising to visit Mercedes. When I didn't, Mercedes came knocking at my door. I followed her and her husband to the car like a duckling, letting them drive me to their house, eating the sardines Alba's father served me with disgust but in politeness, falling asleep in Alba's bed shortly after, and waking up the evening of the following day with a stuffed mothball-smelling white bear under my cheek.

Prompted by Mercedes, I made an appointment with my family physician. She believed that I needed a little push to get on with life, a few months' worth of a magic pill to put things in perspective, to drown the fear. I could then think about what to do or not do next.

A few weeks after I began taking Prozac, I woke up at 5:00 AM with the astonishing urge to call and catch up with everyone in my address book. Looking for the book but not finding it, I grew anxious, light-headed. The thought that I had disappointed everybody sent my heart racing. By the time I found it, I had changed my mind. I wanted to go shopping, cut my hair, join the gym, find a job, fly to Mexico and visit a writer I had met earlier in the year. I wanted to begin writing again, see my husband for an hour or two, and clean the apartment. I was a frantic bundle of energy.

When I told Mercedes I was having dinner with him, she was worried. She wasn't sure if I was ready to face him. He was a wounded man. How was I to handle that? She was right. In the middle of dinner, I stood up and left the restaurant.

When I told her I was going to Mexico, she asked me to wait. I went anyway. When I came back and announced I was going to India with the Mexican writer, she said over her dead body. I stopped seeing her altogether. I didn't go to India. Instead I grew more and more erratic. I ran out of pills. I didn't keep my doctor's appointments. I began to miss him.

I moved in with a man I met in the frozen meat section of a supermarket. I got pregnant for the thirteenth time.

The last time I saw Mercedes was on the street. She was in the passenger seat of a car parked by a mini-market across from my apartment building. I was coming out of the store when I saw the arm of a familiar gray fur coat out the car window, an unlit cigarette dangling at its end. It was December 1998.

Hoping she would not see me, I thought of rushing by, but I couldn't do it. She greeted me with a smile, something she never did. She asked how I was doing and said the extra pounds I had put on were a good thing. I almost told her I was eight weeks pregnant, the first pregnancy with another man, but I thought she didn't deserve my anger, after all.

Her unlit cigarette changed hands a few times while we talked and I finally asked if she needed a light. She said she didn't smoke. Holding a cigarette was just a habit. She was wearing the bracelet I'd given her a decade ago. I missed her. I leaned down and told her so. She pinched my chin. I played with her bracelet while she talked about him. He'd changed, he saw what he'd done wrong, he'd grown modest, he often came by their house, brought her books, he was a good friend.

I felt dizzy. The unyielding Mercedes I'd known, the one who did not smile and had little compassion for people's frailties, the Mercedes whose courage I had wished to borrow just one time even if it had not lasted a day, had receded behind a tenderness that broke her voice at times. She sounded like any other woman.

Against her softness and reason, pregnant as I was and isolated from everything, I felt like an obstinate and unreasonable mess. I kept on playing nervously with her bracelet. With shaking hands I took it off her wrist and put it on mine. Then I tried to take it off, but it wouldn't come loose. In exasperation, I pulled on the clasp and for some reason this pull assumed a vital importance, perhaps because Mercedes was watching so intently and because my ex-husband, out of nowhere, had just gotten into the car and sat behind the wheel.

He had driven her to the pharmacy to pick up her prescriptions. I had not recognized the car. My heart was beating violently. I bent my wrist and tightened the grip on the bracelet and as it finally slid off, it dropped to the ground. I gave the bracelet back to her. Then Mercedes's hand was under my chin, and as she raised my face, I shut my eyes tightly for fear she would see the tears welling up. She stroked my cheek and asked me to call her. I walked away without having looked at or said a word to him.

She lived through another winter, and through my thirteenth and fourteenth abortions. For a while after her death, I saw her in my mind that Christmas Eve, the gray fur coat, her mannerisms, her weak smile, and then I saw her lying in her bed, dead. I often think about her, especially at night, but each time it is the other Mercedes I recall, the one veiled by smoke, warning me against a life of serfdom.

In late April 2002, I flew to Puerto Rico. I had not been back since Miguel's funeral. Two days after my arrival, I woke up alone in a back room that seemed more like a warehouse than a doctor's office, with my ex-husband's voice pushing against the walls of my head. They weren't words exactly but a tone, a warning. Even the two abortions—now three—I had with another man after my divorce felt as if they'd been with him. All around me there were boxes stacked high, dismantled cribs against the wall, and several black garbage bags closed tight. I was terrified at what I had done to myself.

A childhood friend told me about the doctor the day I arrived. In Puerto Rico, abortion was still taboo and most gynecologists preferred not to offer the service in their practice, afraid of chasing away a significant portion of their Catholic, anti-abortion clients. My friend's doctor performed abortion only on his established patients and solely in special circumstances. From what I had told him, I did not meet his criteria. I was using abortion as a method of birth control.

I sat there shocked at how this man's ethics could affect my life. I asked, rhetorically, if I might have to fly back to the States to exercise my right to choose. As I stood up to leave, he apologized for not being able to help me. He asked about my writing. My friend told him I'd published a book. I watched his eyes widen when I told him about my grandmother.

"You're Lolita Lebrón's granddaughter? It can't be!" It was a typical reaction. People in Puerto Rico either adored or hated my grandmother, but there was reverence and awe across the board for this eighty-four-year-old woman's courage, recently arrested and imprisoned yet again for demonstrating against the U.S. Navy in Vieques. He said that for Lolita Lebrón he would do anything.

Feeling an awkward mix of shame and pride, I followed him and a nurse along a dark corridor into a badly lit back room filled with boxes and filing cabinets. It was 8:25 AM by a Mickey Mouse clock hanging on the wall. I was not asked to change into a gown or asked when I had my last period. When I offered this information, he smiled at the nurse. I began to fume at this man's response, but I thought better of upsetting him as he was about to insert a steel speculum inside me. I was told I was eight to ten weeks pregnant. I said it had to be more like twelve.

It was 11:40 when I came to. When I lifted my head off the pillow, the room began to spin. I woke up again at 2:00 PM. The doctor and the nurse were somewhere in the room. I could hear their voices. There had been too much blood, he said. He wanted me to stay overnight. Their voices slowly faded behind my ex-husband's voice, which grew louder until it banged inside my head just as a piercing headache suddenly set in.

"You are locked into repetition, you will be there forever," it yelled.

"But this is not your freaking child," I pleaded back.

"And what's the damn difference?" my own voice betrayed me. "Look at you!"

I got off the bed, but the headache shut my eyes. In the darkness, the room spun even faster.

It was sometime after 4:00 PM when I opened the door to the waiting room and found my father arguing with the receptionist. We walked out to the car in silence, in my father's kind of silence, which is his way of saying if somebody is going to tell a lie, it better be you, because I don't lie. In this, he reminded me of my ex-husband.

Inside the car he said I needed to eat. He drove away humming his usual song about an old horse outrunning his young. He was annoyingly off key.

My father sang and hummed often throughout my childhood, and spoke little. At some point in my adult life I began to resent his nonintrusive demeanor. It was easy to lie to my father. I envied friends in college, mainly Americans, whose parents intruded in their lives, called on the phone, wrote letters, dropped in, and confronted their children if they suspected anything was wrong. My friends would at one point or another say, "I'm sick of my parents." It was shocking that you could speak of your parents that way. Both my mother and father were bigger than life, even in their smallness, in their mistakes.

I knew then that I had never deceived him. He always knew what I was up to but he chose every time to have me carry the burden of the lie or the choice. It wasn't fair. When you care deeply about a daughter you protect her from herself. You give advice, you offer direction, you confront a lie, at the risk of being rejected. You give yourself openly, without reservation. My father did care. It was just that he probably cared more about being who he was than anything else.

He drove me to a restaurant. There I looked out at a beach where I had spent many afternoons playing in the sand while my mother attempted to cover up her marital unhappiness with a man in a car. On that same beach my father and I had bought conchs by the dozens from a toothless fisherman every Thursday. I had played, cried, slept, napped, dreamt, had nightmares, eaten, taken a crap, laughed, fought, imagined myself a ballerina, a dolphin, my own mother, on that beach. The stretch of sand and the sea were still there, but I wasn't.

I took another bite of my conch salad to please my father then threw up on his lap. When I came to, he was carrying me. The sky was tinged by a purplish remnant of gold, and the sea had shadowy hues mixed with wavy patches of faint light. In the car, my father stared at the bottom of a glass filled with white rum. He had a weather-beaten face, aging and tired. "If I had one chance," he said to the glass, "only one chance to change anything in my life, I would not have sent you away at such an early age."

I decided to coldly tell him the details of my fifteenth abortion, and the hard facts of all the previous ones. Words rushed out of me, desperate to reach my father, to shake him loose from both his new benevolent nostalgia and his past indifference. As I told my father the horrors of my private life, details of my life with him and my mother came back to me. I could see the present take a shape, the shape of my past. I saw it was me, after all, who had not stayed put long enough for my father to relate to me. I had turned my back on him, my family, my country. I had become an amorphous woman, a partial person. Born of this simple man by my side, in this Spanish-speaking island, I had quickly changed my whole outlook on the world as a result of a life that took me away from all this.

In response to everything I had said, my father took his newspaper from the dashboard and opened it to the sports section. I watched in disbelief. At some point, he carefully folded the newspaper and closed his eyes. He appeared to be asleep, but then he opened his eyes and looked straight at me with eyes so clear and lit with compassion that I knew he was seeing everything: not just me, and not just my mother, twenty-five years in the past, but into the future, too. The question my father asked felt to me like a tender caress, an embrace of understanding:

"How is it my daughter has had to suffer like this? Where the hell have I been?"

I saw my father's little girl, tracing the chain of humiliations, wishing to find an answer to his question. But she quickly shrunk in my eyes, became a child intent on too big a task and set for failure. I was sorry for her. I asked myself: How is it she has had to suffer like this, where the hell have I been?

There was no going back.

Three days later, I had severe abdominal pains. At times, it was so excruciating I folded over and had to catch my breath. After diagnosing an infection and telling me there was fetal tissue yet to be evacuated, my cousin's gynecologist in San Juan performed a D & C. I left the office around three o'clock, worried sick for my brother Fonso, who had been waiting for me at a bus stop since 1:00 PM. I had no way of letting him know I would be late.

I had looked forward to this meeting ever since I landed on the island. In the eight years since my brother Miguel's death, my oldest brother had joined over a dozen rehab programs and quit them all within a week. We had talked on the phone once or twice a year and in these brief conversations, when he was usually in a drug-induced rush of energy, I had come to know of my brother's big dreams of change, the strain of his wounded dignity on his crushed ego, and finally, toward the end, when he barely could keep up with a minute-long chat, the imminent danger of losing him for good.

I didn't know what I could do, but I knew that I had to spend time with my brother.

He was still there waiting for me. I saw him before he saw me. Pacing alongside an empty bench, he kicked one foot against the side of it, and then the other. He seemed to be trying to get rid of something stuck to his shoe or the hem of his pants. Then he did the same thing with his hands, and I called out to him.

Inside the car, he was sweating profusely and kept shaking his feet loose of something. I asked if he was feeling all right. "I just have a stomach virus," he said, pointing at the traffic and behind us, desperate to take us out of there.

"Where should we eat?" I asked.

His shoulders began to shake. I put a hand on his back. His skeletal over-six-feet-tall frame bent forward on the seat. He had dark, violet shadows under sunken eyes. As he tried to speak, he yawned and then again, and again. In between yawns, he said, "I'm freezing. Can you shut off the air conditioning?"

He was staring at his feet, begging me to drive away, when he let out a cry of pain followed by vomit.

Coming from a family with two brothers afflicted by heroin addiction you would think I knew better.

"We have to go to a hospital," I said.

"I'm sorry Irene, I'm sorry . . ." He shook his head and yawned.

"I shouldn't have stopped," he said, "not now, when I was going to see my little sister."

"How long has it been?" I asked him.

"Two days and if I don't get a fix right now I'm going to die."

He said these words while opening the car door. I pulled him back by the shirt collar. His frail body was malleable; it fell on me. He didn't resist. I understood my brother was in major withdrawal.

"Just give me a few minutes," I tried to comfort him. "I'll get you to an emergency room in no time."

He couldn't go to a hospital. They would give him methadone. He couldn't survive on methadone. He'd rather jump out of the car to his death before going to a hospital.

He began to sob violently and then stopped. His sudden calm scared me.

"I know a place you can take me not far from here." He spoke softly, the shaking gone. "I can get cured this one time and then I'll plan better to leave this shit for good, I promise you Irene, you will never see me like this ever again, it's not far and I won't even use a needle, I can snort it and be done with it."

His legs began to shake again.

"You can wait for me, I'll be fine and we can talk then, but look at me now."

I feared his composure was like the eye of a hurricane, and the worst side of the storm was about to come. I saw an opening on my right and cut across to the emergency lane. I pressed the gas, put the emergency lights on, and asked my brother where was this cure of his.

He came back when he said he would, in twenty minutes. I was waiting for him in a restaurant. I saw him cross the street with quick steps, his body erect, much taller than I'd thought he was. He said good afternoon to the street vendor on the sidewalk and stopped to help an old man park his car. Then he turned to the bar looking for me. When our eyes met he pointed at the sky. A hot air balloon was above us, an orange rooster drawn on it.

"That's Dad up there, you know," he said, sitting at the small table brimming with three plates of Mexican food I ordered for him.

"The rooster, that's Dad's nickname." I knew that, of course. "And mine too," he went on, staring at the food on the table, "mine too."

His speech was slowing down, slurring. He looked at me as he took a bite of the enchilada and then gagged. His pupils seemed odd, tiny and sharp.

"How can I help you Fonsito, please tell me."

I saw his eyelids droop, his head nod. I asked him to rest on my lap. He sighed and like an obedient little child, laid his right cheek on me and nodded off.

The next few hours I saw my brother Miguel many times. I saw him high up on a tree reaching for the first ripe guava of summer and then kneeling down by me, biting off the rotten parts of the fruit until it was just perfect. I saw him sneaking into my room at night, crawling very slowly toward my piggy bank on the night table. His hand was working at it, trying to pry it open when I asked if he would scratch my back until I fell asleep. He put the piggy bank on the night table and pushed a few bills into it out of guilt, the ones he'd probably just stolen from dad, before lying next to me. I saw him running to the back of the house and coming up front, water hose in hand and yelling for Mom to spray me free of fire ants. I saw him getting them off with his own hands when the water didn't come on and then carrying me on his back across the lawn, pretending he was a horse, until my tears dried off. I saw him sitting on the steps of our house in Palmas Altas the day after my mother's funeral. His face was pressed between his hands and he didn't hear me crying out to him for help, stuck high up in a tree.

After that, his image blurred. I remembered the day in 1992 when I saw him last at a bus stop and he ran out on me, and the time at his own funeral, when I saw what was left of my dear brother disappear under the white marble of a grave's lid.

I caressed Fonsito's forehead, praying his fate would be different, asking myself why it seemed we had all been damned. How was my life different from theirs? I was seemingly the success story, gone to college early, done well in my studies, married a professor, led a life of boating, academia, writing. Yet, here I was, cushioning my brother's misery with my own, trying to mother him with a body that only three days before had yet again been ransacked by my own madness.

If my brother wished he could cease to be who he was for me, I wished I could do the same.

The day before I flew back to New York, I went back to Caracoles Beach and sat on the sand looking out to sea. I gazed down at my bare legs burning under the sun: they were the legs of a different woman. I had lost the body I'd had since childhood.

Later that day, I asked my father to take me to the house I grew up in. He said a fire had burned most of the structure down, the site was covered with tall grass, and I wouldn't get through. "You'll get bitten by rats or rabid dogs roaming the grounds." When he stopped the car on the side of the road farther from the house, I asked why he wouldn't park closer and he pinched his nose warning me against the smell.

"You shouldn't go out there," he said staring at the wheel. "The town turned the front yard into a junkyard and a dump for dead pets. There is nothing there, believe me," he pleaded, "better remember it in its good old days."

But I didn't want to remember as much as I wanted to forget. I got out of the car and, for the first time since I was twelve years old, went past the entrance gate that was no longer there. There was no path and the grass stung my bare knees. The ground was covered by deep layers of garbage, toilets, half tubs, rusted engines, birdcages, land-crab traps, mufflers, a fridge with rotten food in it. I climbed over an unusually big fake Christmas tree and, balancing on an oven, jumped over a swamp-like area of the yard. I was getting closer when the smell struck with such force I gagged. Next to my left foot a dog's paw lay close to my big toe. Flies hovered above and around his limp, brown body and all the others lying along the swamp.

Father was waving for me to return to the car. I kept digging through the garbage. The same tamarind trees still stood and towered over the house on each side. The twisting branches cast a net of shadow. All I could see was giant-sized tamarinds with small, dry leaves of no special color surrounding what was left of the house.

The last time I'd driven by, eight or so years before, the uninhabited house had already been touched by the galloping decay of the tropics. I had refused to get out of the car and instead watched the many dogs sleeping on the front balcony and lying in the tall grass under the shade of the tamarind trees. The decay and the weight of memory seemed less against the backdrop of these new residents and the generous canopy of trees blocking the burning sun from their backs.

Now, fire had found its way in and made of my origins a concrete block with blackened window openings, peering out at the world, with the impassive look of death. And just as I had needed to come closer to my mother's body at her funeral and touch her nose, I needed to go back into the house, no matter how little was left. I went up the cement steps, walked the length of the balcony, and noticed a small lizard in between the tiles of the floor. I had spent whole days on that balcony looking at lizards, betting on which way they would go when I came close.

The rooms were still divided and I entered each one and closed my eyes. In the darkness I saw the past come to life, heard the frightening sounds of night, the happy ones of daybreak, my father's old rooster I pretended one summer was a puppy. I smelled something like cilantro, then it was a foul, sulfuric stench coming from the shower, rising from the drain. I felt the furry white coat of my hamster Figaro snuggled against the side of my neck, and I felt the rain, the rain pouring down on my face while I ran through the backyard chasing land crabs.

In my parents' bedroom, the rainbow my brother Cheo had painted between the two windows facing the sea wasn't there any longer. On the bottom right of the cement window frame there was a wasp's nest. But behind it, at the corner of the opening, a hint of blue, red, and maybe green, a smudge of color, showed through the dirt. It was my brother's rainbow.

I walked back to the car. The sun was setting. At some point I took a last look. Color was draining from the sky, leaving a faint violet smear against which the house stood out even more clearly in all its demise. I turned my back to it and drove away thankful the house was still there.

Daylight vanished quickly. I'd forgotten that about my homeland. Stars flashed one after another as we drove past the landscape of my childhood. I opened the window. In the fields surrounding the house the tiny frogs only found in Puerto Rico, the coqui, began their incessant chorus, which steadily grew louder as the evening cooled off. I expected to be nostalgic, touched, and yet the feeling was one of waste, a feeling that this one space, the place I lived in as a child, was one among hundreds of spaces that had multiplied, been broken up. If there was continuity to it all, a landmark that remained unchanged, it was right next to me. It was my father.

"What did you see?" he asked.

"Cantabrico," I said. "I could hear him clearly in the back porch as if he was still there." Father let out a happy chuckle.

"Ah, Cantabrico, poor old rooster, and to think he was your first dog, with a leash and all!" We laughed together.

Your past is the situation you are no longer in, wrote Simone de Beauvoir.

But is it?

It was a cool, sunny June back in Syracuse. I spent more days and evenings at the apartment I had rented the previous fall but seldom used because I felt uncomfortable being alone and was unable to end the relationship with my boyfriend. One afternoon, shortly after I returned from Puerto Rico, he removed my sweater and my bra. I glanced down at my drooping, shrunken breasts, swollen with a pregnancy only two months before. Suddenly I was angry. I put my clothes back on and left, uncertain of what or whom I was angry at.

I began to write in earnest. I woke up in the morning and headed straight to my computer. I read and wrote or stared at the base of my oak cabinet, which sheltered me from the life of a writer I was still reluctant to join. Some evenings I had dinner with my boyfriend, watched his pleasure in eating, how he punctuated every other bite with a shot of vodka, listened to his majestic plans of success for the symphony piece he had been working on for most of his adult life, other plans of making it big in the stock market when he found the investor to back him up, and so on.

I listened, asking myself why on earth I had shared any part of my life with this adult child who hadn't worked a day since I'd known him; I wished the tenderness and lightheartedness that had originally attracted me had been followed by a responsible man I could admire. He complained that I wasn't paying attention to what he was saying. Soon he had other complaints. My editing work at the university press and the writing were stiffening me, turning me into a dutiful, career-oriented American woman. I went to bed with him, dreading his alcohol breath on my forehead, his big, white body on me.

He wanted a baby. Finally a man shared in my maternal desire. I had become pregnant by him three times. All three times, I came close to choosing to become a single mother. He resented the abortions. He called me selfish and insensitive. I was tempted to marry him on a few occasions, to give form to a life that felt amorphous and without direction. I stopped myself.

In July I went to Bennington, Vermont, to attend my second of the MFA writing workshops I had started the January before. The first day, my teacher, Susan Cheever, had taken me to Robert Frost's grave.

"I try to bring as many of my students as I can," she said leaning against a twisted maple.

"Now, what's with this Pygmalion story you are writing? I don't get it. I smell rat all over this love story of yours." She squatted next to her dog and began stroking his furry back.

"I had twelve abortions in eleven years with my ex-husband and they were the happiest years of my life," I said. Not one word of what I was saying sounded familiar to me. It was as if it was someone else's life I was referring to.

"Well, there you have it, girl."

"But I don't know what I'm saying," I said. I felt there was no story to tell beyond that one crazy sentence.

She grabbed my hand and started up the hill to the car, turning to point at Frost's grave below. "I tell you, that man never lets me down."

By the end of the workshop, I knew the task ahead of me was to give up my idealized memory.

But a whole year would go by before, under the right circumstances, in the strange land of self-reflection, my memory ripped open so that I could see "the happiest years of my life" as the story of an abortion addict.

Back in Syracuse, I sent for my sisters. Diana was now nineteen years old, Miri eighteen, and I couldn't take my eyes off them, even though I'd seen them earlier that summer. I had last shared any significant amount of time with them in 1995, when they lived aboard *Sarabande* with us for most of the summer. Then, they were simply two girls enthralled by their big sister's life, including her husband, whom they were afraid of bothering with their laughter.

I picked them up at the airport and drove them straight to my own boat. *Second Wind* was not *Sarabande*. After the divorce, I had roamed the shores of Lake Ontario dreaming of boats and of sailing around the world, the only thing I could picture doing by myself. I found her in a rundown boatyard in Sodus Point. As old as she was, she was a Bristol sloop with amazingly dry decks and a deep, full keel, twenty-eight feet long and weathered. I bought *Second Wind* with my one thousand dollar tax refund.

I took my sisters across the lake to Kingston and taught them how to sail. We anchored off state parks and camped ashore. We caught fish and cooked them right over the campfire. We hiked along high cliffs. We did things I had not dared do alone.

One evening while we slept on shore, the wind blew strong and I feared the anchor could drag. I tried to get the dinghy in the water so I could motor to the boat and throw a second anchor, but the waves would not let me launch it. Before I could decide what to do next, Diana swam to the boat and Miri followed behind. They set the second anchor and swam back. I looked at my sisters shocked that I did not know them well, and that I had not cared for their love all those years, or the love of my family for that matter. It struck me, the poverty of my life.

On my thirty-third birthday, the day before they were leaving, I took them to a spa for a facial and a massage, a full makeover. We went shopping and took a long walk along the Erie Canal. We dressed up and drove to a five-star restaurant on Skaneateles Lake. We each ate something we had never eaten. Diana had frog legs, Miri, venison, I, ostrich. We fell asleep on my bed cuddled together under a big down blanket.

The day they left, I broke up with my boyfriend and moved back to my apartment. For weeks I did nothing but work on writing packets for an upcoming winter residency at Bennington. Every morning and every night I walked my dog Oliveira. I saw he was growing weak in his old age. One day his knees gave way and he fell on his face. I called my ex-boyfriend. By late August I was back in a wrong relationship. My dog of fifteen years was dying, but I wouldn't see it.

Earlier in the year, Oliveira had begun to grow frail. It began with the water. Each time I filled his bowl, he drank it down in a frenzy. Running to the bowl, he banged into the kitchen wall and banged himself again when he stood back up. One morning, he dipped his whole face in the bowl and almost drowned. The vet said he had cataracts and his kidneys were growing old. The doctor prescribed a senior diet, but Oliveira lost interest in food and grew more obsessed with water. I found him desperately licking the base of the refrigerator for hours. I grew mad. I yelled at him, but he went on as if he had grown deaf too. He abandoned his bed and moved into the kitchen, under a radiator; there he sank into an unnerving wait for water and watched for flies. In his seafaring days, he had snapped at them.

Shortly after my sisters left, the accidents began. I put a gate in the kitchen. One night I found pee and poop all over the kitchen floor and walls. I could see the imprint where Oliveira had bumped against a corner or wedged himself and tried frantically to find his way out. I felt my fear give way to an anger I'd never known.

"Stop falling, stop drinking water like a maniac, stop with the accidents."

I howled these absurdities at my poor dog. I felt a deep shame. He managed to stand up. I came closer. He started toward me, but took a sharp left toward a cabinet and bumped into his food bowl, tipping it over and spreading the tiny dry morsels across the floor. "Enough!" I knocked him down with my voice. And he, bellowing in astonishment and fear, slipped again, swerving sideways and bumping into the radiator. Then he rolled over on his back and held his paws up. I sat on the kitchen floor and wept.

I took him to a different vet, who told me Oliveira had a slow-growing tumor on his left back leg. His liver enzymes were off balance and his kidneys were failing. After a weeklong hospitalization, he was stabilized, but his legs shook when he walked and he often fell on his side when he lifted his back paw to pee. He began to pee sitting down.

I grew distant. I began to look away each time I walked by the gated kitchen. Three days after he returned home, I left him at a kennel while I went for a last sail of the season on Lake Ontario with my boyfriend. We were stranded in Toronto for days waiting for the weather to clear. When we finally sailed into the Oswego harbor in the middle of a thunderstorm, I realized Oliveira had been neglected for eight days. I found him in a corner of his cage, unconscious. Flies hovered above his eyes. I thought I had killed him.

On the hour-long drive to the veterinary hospital I rocked my dog's limp body in my arms; some of my tears fell onto his sloping forehead, the others into my hand. At the hospital I was told Oliveira would not live through the night. I could spare the dog and myself some pain if he was put to sleep. I simply couldn't do it. He would have to die in my arms. Next day, a Monday, he was still alive. I rushed him to a vet at Cornell Veterinary Hospital. He stayed there for two days. When I got him back, he couldn't walk or feed himself. I was told he had anywhere from seventy-two hours to a couple of weeks to live; it was all up to him and my care. I took him away with an IV hooked to his right front paw and a box filled with medicines and IV replacements. I was to attempt feeding him every two hours around the clock and give him physical therapy six times a day. There was hope he might move his head to the point he could eat again on his own, perhaps even sit up.

During the cruelest or scariest moments in life, when I have felt the most debased, I have found a fierce need to see myself rising up to the challenge.

I carried Oliveira to church wrapped in a blanket. Kneeling before a virgin cast in bronze, I prayed and begged this virgin I had not cared about since I was twelve years old and lonely in boarding school to have my dog stay alive a little longer. For three Sundays, I walked into mass with Oliveira's limp body nestled in my arms and begged even harder.

Every time I succeeded in getting an eyedropper full of food down Oliveira's mouth or found the tiniest speck of bowel movement in his makeshift diaper, I thought, "My dog ought to be dead and yet he is not." Each minute felt like a narrow escape. At night when Oliveira moaned himself to sleep on my chest, I couldn't decide whether I had reached the limits of horror or beauty.

Every day I carried him in his bed to the park and set him in the grass. He snoozed in the sun. I petted him, fed him, watched him sleep, followed the clouds blowing across the sky. One cold Friday night in late September, I took him to *Second Wind.* In the V-berth, I listened to the wind rock the boat. Oliveira was warm and his front legs stretched across my shoulder. He buried his drippy nose into my neck and blew little snot bubbles. I felt his back paws kicking, his nose twitching rapidly. My dog was dreaming, could still dream.

I spent five thousand dollars trying to get what the vet believed would be a few days or weeks of life. I got a month and a half. I understood Milan Kundera's words: "Mankind's true moral test consists of its attitude toward those who are at its mercy: animals." It was true. My morality was suspect. No remorse or amount of money toward my dog's medical care could change that.

On October 6, 2002, while Oliveira was still alive, I was supposed to leave for Spain to meet my father and his four siblings to attend the wedding of a cousin and a gathering of relatives whom I had not seen since I left there as a thirteen-year-old. From Spain, I would go to the Frankfurt Book Fair on behalf of my editing job at a university press. If I left, I would probably be saying good-bye to Oliveira. My ex-husband, whom I'd called when I first was told Oliveira would die at any moment, and who had remained in touch ever since, loved Oliveira deeply and had made a short movie about him, had written an essay, a poem, and a story about him. Giving Oliveira up when we split had been painful.

Two days before I was scheduled to leave and already having made up my mind to stay, I met him at a campus bagel shop. He watched me feed Oliveira, who was wrapped in a woolen blanket. For the first time, Oliveira took all three eyedroppers of food and five of water. Just as he finished his last little gulp he lifted his head more than he had since he'd fallen ill, and looked up toward his former master. Since he could not move his limbs much, he was stuck in place with only his head wobbling up in the air between us. I could not say no to the tearful man sitting across me when he asked if I could please share Oliveira's last days with him.

On October 12, my first morning at the book fair, six days after leaving Oliveira at his apartment with a three-page list of nursing chores, my cell phone showed a call from his telephone number. I found a corner in a crowded hallway and dialed. He was on his way to the vet. His voice broke. Oliveira was on his lap. He had eaten all his food the night before, almost a two-meal serving, had almost stood up on his four legs after he'd given him the evening's physical therapy session, had even lifted his left ear in excitement at his sweet-tasting liquid multivitamins. The dog fell asleep nestled on his stomach and did not moan once in the night. In the morning, he'd had a big, healthy bowel movement, but then Oliveira would not wake up. He knew the dog was dead.

Walking down those crowded hallways of the fair, trying to find the Quebec collective's publishing booth, my life felt full of meaningless activity. I sat with a Canadian publisher, originally from Haiti, and discussed possible co-editions and books we loved. The more things in common we found, the less able I was to hold back the tears. At some point, just as he was describing one peculiar fruit that grew in the northeastern coast of Haiti where he was from, I began to cry. I excused myself and went to the bathroom. Back at the booth he did not ask a question and went on with his story. The tears came back. When we continued talking I told him my dog had died. And this man, who for some part of the meeting I had felt a brother, simply from an island over in the Caribbean, did not say a thing. I was mad. I asked what was with him; why wouldn't he say he was sorry, pat me on the shoulder, or say anything?

"Forgive me," he said, staring blankly into my eyes. "I do not have any love for dogs."

Before I could say to him, "So what is your problem?" he pulled his chair over closer to mine and said:

"It is hard for a man to have any sympathy for the death of a dog when half his relatives were bitten to death by packs of them, all trained to perfection by Papa Doc's secret police."

It couldn't be. I tried to speak. I had nothing to say.

"I watched from up a tree. Below me the Tonton Macoutes led the dogs on and fed them treats of raw meat."

Riding the train back to the hotel, the story of the Haitian man played back in my mind. I felt my pain at Oliveira's death settle quietly in a corner of my heart.

When I got to my room I called my father. He asked me to pour myself a drink from the minibar, cognac preferably, and to come back to the phone. Then he said the lives of dogs were brief and yet our feeling toward them could be everlasting. It was a predicament. But I should know that because metabolic rates differ on the same scale as size and longevity, a mouse will experience as many heartbeats during its brief lifetime as an elephant with its long life. Everyone, he told me with a chuckle that bothered me, gets roughly the same share. My dog got himself a brief life or a long one, depending on how I looked at it.

I was taken aback by my father's dismissive words, and by his uncharacteristic use of so many of them to soothe me. And as I told him the story of the Haitian man, I understood my father was not the right person to have called. When I picked up the phone to call my ex-husband, I changed my mind. He wasn't right either. Instead, I curled up in bed and wept. I grew calmer. My calm was made of resignation.

• • •

I drove straight to the vet from the airport. The nurse handed me a black garbage bag with the frozen body of my dog in it, a condolence card stapled to the top. I sat behind the wheel of my car with the heavy bag on my lap. For six weeks, I had driven everywhere with Oliveira's feather-like body on me. I had grown so attuned to his feel that I could tell if his weight changed from ride to ride. As much as I tried to connect the dog in the bag with the dog I loved, I couldn't put the two together. I rushed to a nearby park and buried Oliveira in a silk, yellow dress on the south side of a boat ramp by a small lake.

As I dug the shovel into the frozen ground, I thought of my mother's burial. Her coffin had been wrapped in the Puerto Rican nationalist flag. To think that for most of my life, I had forgotten the love of a mother, yet, remembered it, felt it again, in Oliveira's eyes. It was as if in tending to Oliveira, I was given the chance to see her come back after she abandoned me, and feel all the remorse, all the love, and want nothing else but to repair what she'd destroyed. I had left my dog in a kennel for over a week blind to the fact he needed me, that he was frail and dying. I was his whole world. My mother left me too, blind to the fact I could not live without her. She was my whole world. It baffles me to this day how by coming to be so delicately known by my dog, I felt my mother's love revive in me, if for a brief period. I saw how at some moment or another we could be capable of unthinkable neglect. I felt empathy for my mother then, saw that she would have cared for me had she had a second chance.

Two days after I buried Oliveira, I saw my former master for the last time. Over dinner at his favorite restaurant, I would say something and he would reply: "Didn't I teach you that?"

He was eating a pickle. "Your love/hate relationship with your reproductive system killed our love story. That and the writing . . . It is all my fault," he said. "I should have given you a child. I should not have told you to write." He put the pickle down.

I could see love in his eyes. It should have surprised me, pleased me, and yet all I felt was pity for the lamb I had made of him.

Caring for a dying dog does remarkable things to you, he said. But why did I take away from him the opportunity to bury Oliveira along with me? Oliveira was our dog, the dog of our story.

I listened to him answer for me, something he often did. I watched the way he nodded each time he paused and thought about something, his manner of staring off at a place behind me when what I said did not please him.

I told him I picked up my dog from the veterinarian's freezer and buried him myself because I wanted my grief to be only mine and Oliveira's. It was my story.

He stood up and called for the waiter. I took a gulp of wine, wishing I could love him again, wishing I could love at all. As he put a few bills on the table, he said his last words of the evening: He should have given me that child. What irony. To know now a child could have saved me from the bitter, middle-aged woman I had become. It was all his fault. He was sorry for me. He should never have forced me to write, to make his life easier. He should have never placed such a burden on my ego. I would never be able to write another book without him.

In my car, driving back to an apartment filled with packing boxes, I heard the voice of my newfound, little self pushing me along, "Take to the road. And don't turn back: It's not worth it."

My heart was vacant and for the first time since I was fourteen years old I was not attached to a man in any significant way. It was

a liberating yet somewhat hopeless situation. But I took the lone-
liness and fear of the unknown a thousand times over the prison
of the symbiotic, one-and-only relationships I'd frantically built
throughout the years.

One morning my father woke me with the news that my brother
Fonso had completed twelve weeks of detox and rehabilitation at
a hospital in New Jersey and was graduating to a new program that
would last through May. My father wanted us all to visit my brother
over Christmas. He gave me the telephone number.

"I promised you, Irenita," Fonso said. "Do you remember? I
made a promise to my sister and I kept it."

There had been so many promises, I couldn't really tell.

"Don't think that way," I said. "Don't pressure yourself with
promises. I love you no matter what." I feared he was just like me
and I didn't want him to set himself up for failure.

"Listen, when I let you see the worm I'd become that day you
took me to La Perla, I hit bottom. There was nothing left to do
but to die for good or prove to my little sister life should not be
the way I'd showed her."

My brother had been a substance abuser and a heroin addict
for over two decades. Everyone had given him up for dead. Only
my dad had kept vigil, resigned. "No one is dead until he is dead
and buried deep down under," my grandmother Irene always said.

I was in the shower chasing a bar of soap around up the corners of the tub and thinking I did not want to die. That morning a gynecologist told me I could develop cervical cancer. The dye they spread on my cervix had lit up the entire surface of the tissue. It was almost blinding. She didn't look at me when she said that 20 percent of cervical neoplasia would progress to cervical cancer if left untreated. I had to follow up as soon as the final lab results arrived. HSIL could not be taken lightly. A nurse came in, pointing to the window.

It was the first snow of winter. The gynecologist smiled and excused herself. She would be back in a few minutes to answer any questions. Before she closed the door, she said it could all be an error.

I didn't wait for her to return. Outside, the snow came down in thick, heavy globs and hung on the trees. It made the world seem soft and lovely. That the world I was in could be soft and lovely was more than I could bear, so I stood there, facing college students rushing between classes, and wept. I didn't want to die.

At home, I fell asleep the moment I sat on the couch. When I woke up, it was dark. I remembered the doctor's office, but stopped myself from thinking. Take a shower. Eat. Have a glass of wine. Then think. I had learned to repress with style.

But then a bar of soap forced me to the ground. I had finally caught the soap with both hands when I slipped and fell face first against the tub. I lay there contemplating my fall as the proper ending to a period of my life. It was the first time I had been confronted with the real possibility of death.

From where I lay and through the plastic shower curtain, I could see the little picture frame of my therapist, Joan, that I had hung by the bathroom mirror when she moved away. I hung it there to remind myself each morning of the hard work we had accomplished. But I had not noticed the picture in a long while. I thought tenderly of her and just as I made a move to get out of the tub to finally call her after months of dreading to pick up the phone, I thought: "You get out of here. You do that first, then you call her."

I made a promise to myself. I had to leave Syracuse. It was a promise without a deadline, I just had to commit myself and then forget the whole thing, letting faith, a basic trust in life's renewable resources, make known when the time was ripe. I closed myself up in my apartment, writing to forget I was mortal.

In my last session with Joan, we looked back at my progress, how my grief, which had been gridlocked, had become more fluid in the last year. How my emphasis in therapy began to change. Instead of talking about my ex-husband I came to spend long sessions describing my life story. I remembered my childhood in Palmas Altas differently from the one I had recalled when writing about it in my memoir.

We discovered that the distance I put between my country and family and myself for close to two decades had not been all his doing. Escape was my solution to coping with the harsh facts of life, the inevitability of death, freedom to make my life my ultimate aloneness. I chose him. I made him the runway of my flight. I owned him as much as I owned my dreams and my nightmares.

I learned too that my pain was not very different from Joan's and anybody else's; the difference lay in the fact that I had lost a parent, and when one loses a parent, one loses one's past.

Right from the start she asked what about him was so lovable. I said he'd never lied and that all he said was in tune with a higher truth, one that came from being courageous enough to be different, to be the leader of his own destiny, even if at the cost of success and recognition, which meant he was beyond vanity and ego and narcissism and would rather die unknown and without one possession than join the rat race and pay with his freedom, et cetera, et cetera. It became clear that I believed I lacked those qualities I found admirable in him. Joan pointed out that I knew about these qualities, in great part, because I had heard him articulate them himself. It was true he lived his life accordingly, but he had taught me why I should love him.

"But don't we all teach the other how and why to love us?" I asked her.

She said: "Some teach better than others and you suck at it."

His life was the art of gazing at his life, and teaching others how to do the same. It had all been a grand thing, for a while. In therapy, he became a profile, created out of my answers to Joan.

"To love is tiresome, isn't it?" she asked me. "But is perhaps preferable to not loving at all."

It was not a question, nor a common statement but more like thinking aloud, sharing a private thought. I was grateful for Joan's confidence. I could love, yet I didn't have to. Either way, there was something to be gained.

Joan would bring me to a place where I was free to postpone everything, where there was no reason or need to act out. In some comic way, she encouraged me to never do today what I could leave for tomorrow. In fact, I needed not to do anything at all, tomorrow or today. I was to endure turning inward and staring at my fears in the face. I was to not think about what I was going to do with my day or with my life. I had run on survival mode for too long, moving constantly and acting out my fears to exhaustion.

I was to live my paralysis, not be lived by it. I was to be my own depressive self. Such were her instructions. I slept days away, no longer in despair of being nothing and failing to do anything of value.

In one session she began with the question: "What do you want?" At first, I disliked the question, found it simplistic, incapable of bringing anything fruitful to the session. But I was quickly surprised to hear a long list of wants crowd up my mind. What was more shocking was that each one was impossible to fulfill. So much wanting, so much pain, baffled me. I wanted to go back in time, I wanted to stop time, I wanted my mother back, I wanted Miguel back, I wanted a love that does not die, I wanted to merge, fuse, forever and not be unhappy about it. All the wants were enveloped by the sentiment that I should have done more or done things differently. I was ridden with guilt, a condition Joan saw as a profound human wish to control the uncontrollable. If I was guilty about not having done something that I should have done, then it followed that there was something that could have been done; a comforting thought that distracts from my helplessness.

For months after that one session, I brought up a new concern almost every time we met. It felt I was growing disorganized in my pain. My complaints were varied but came down to the same fear. I can't be alone. I won't ever be able to love again. I want the love for my ex-husband back. Maybe I'm simply not in love, but still love him. I feel remorse all the time. I can't organize a thought. My mind is engaged in a hopeless, thoughtless, obsessive decorating habit. I can't keep a promise, much less an appointment. I can't return a phone call. I can't get myself to do anything productive, I can't leave the man I am living with. I know he's the wrong man. I can't write. My ex-husband is right. I will never be able to write another book. I am pregnant again.

I apologized for being unable to sustain focus.

"You are courageously unfolding a multilayered grief," she said. "I'm only here to help you realize what must be done and then trust your own desire for growth and change."

What I needed to do grew clearer the more loyal to our relationship I became. I was to assert my freedom and responsibility by self-assertion no matter the anxiety. I had to emerge or merge, separate or embed. I was to become my own parent or remain the eternal child.

It was not a real choice. I was in therapy because I didn't want to die of fear. I had to learn to live with the dead, and for that I first had to learn to live with the living. Going back home was long overdue.

In our last session she sent me off reminding me of the radical experiences that had shattered the illusion of fusion I longed for at all times. She confronted me with the unbridgeable gap between myself and others. My mother, Miguel, Mercedes, my ex-husband. Melting into another person was no longer possible. My masters were as fragile and finite as I was. My questions and my search for meaning could only be satisfied through work and love.

Out in the streets of downtown Syracuse I stared up at the building where I had met three times a week for over two years with a sixty-something-year-old woman, who often had to fight dozing off mid-session. I was amazed that I had overcome my doubts about her and stayed. I was grateful. Her soothing voice had become a part of me, and with it I had begun soothing my frantic inner child, mainly by saying to her, "Stay put, no need to run, no need to escape or hide." Now she was retiring from practice and moving to Florida with her husband. I was staying behind to clean up my life.

I resolved to leave Syracuse by year's end. I wanted the ocean nearby and snow to keep me in, turned inward, as I committed myself, finally, to a writing life. I found a small granite island off the coast of Maine with an old house facing the harbor.

I lived in a sort of moral intoxication, dazed, aware that I was about to be set free, delivered from the Irene I had ceased to be, but unsure of exactly when and how. On my way to the car one day, I looked closely at the buildings, noticing the date when one was built, and that some had names engraved on their facades. Then I found myself making inventories of the people around me, furniture, clothes, jewelry, animals, temperature. I began noticing walls. I realized there were fourteen walls in my very small apartment. I had no idea I lived among so many walls. I was experiencing a sharpening of my senses, almost psychotic: I noticed soap holders, toilet covers, vanity mirrors, shower-curtain rings, the ways rugs met the wall, key holes. I felt I hadn't seen a thing in my entire life.

January 17, 2003. I had dinner at a Bennington writers' residency with a teacher in whose workshop I had shown the partial manuscript of this book. He told me what he thought.

"Evil is at the center of your story," he said.

I heard him loud and clear. "Your ex-husband's selfishness is evil, but what is most evil, you created him."

After dinner, I went into the café I had avoided for most of the residency choosing to write at night rather than socialize. I was obsessed, too, with my move to Maine the following week, chuckling at how, for the first time in my adult life, I was certain I did not need to love or be loved by a man. That's when he walked in the door.

I was sitting at the end of an old couch watching fellow students dance alone to Latin music. Two women partnered and tried a few salsa steps. I was called to help. On my way back I saw him standing behind the couch. I said hi. He said:

"It's a lonely sight to watch a man dance by himself."

"Would you like to dance?" I asked him.

"Of course," he said.

At first, our conversation went around the wallet pictures of his two children and anecdotes about family gatherings at their mountain home in Colorado. He had a brother and a sister, and among the three of them, six children. He liked to light up a cigar and watch them grow.

"I want kids," I said.

I wanted to go on, to say how I wanted to sit at a writing desk in a little study, the walls lined with shelves holding all the books I treasure, in a little home that was right on the water, with the warm body of a sleeping baby on my lap.

"It must be difficult to write the book you are writing," he said.

"How do you know what I'm working on?"

"I heard you at the readings the other night, the piece about the multiple abortions you'd had." He spoke softly. "I couldn't bear an abortion. That's how I first became a parent. The pain you must have gone through, time after time, I just can't fathom."

"It's difficult to say. I don't know." Slow dancing music began to play. "Do you want to dance again?" I asked him.

"Of course," he said.

Back in our dorm, I fetched my own set of family pictures, mainly pictures from Christmas when I had visited Fonso at the rehab center. Most had my father and all of his five children posing in a corner of my brother's small room. Miguel was missing. I told Dan about Miguel. He told me about his own losses. He'd been married for ten years and was now raising his children, a six-year-old boy and an eleven-year-old girl, on his own. This is how our night went, sharing the wounds and entanglements of our lives, as if we had to establish right off the bat the condition of our hearts.

In the early morning, I woke up curled to the shape of his body, feeling the broad plane of his chest on my back. I lingered in that embrace, awake, until dawn gave way to a bright sunny morning. Later in the day, after class, I waited in my room for his phone call. Finally I called him. He invited me to join him in his afternoon nap. What I thought was an excuse was the truth. He needed to nap. I lay next to him wrapped in his arms as I felt his body relax in sleep and his steady breath warm my cheek. The aggressive, pursuing passion or desire I was accustomed to in men had little to do with him. He seemed firmly anchored in a sense of his own timing, his needs, his rituals, like this peaceful nap, the repose he had promised his body and would not betray for a woman or a fuck or some transitory feeling.

I sat on the bed and looked out the window. The day was sinking and wild hares ran through the snow from tree to tree. I looked at him nap and saw that special smile as he slept. His smile said: *No need to say or do. I'm just fine. You do your thing. It's fun to be alone.* I was thinking of Paul Tillich's new being. I thought of how loyalty to oneself was what I most needed for myself. I was getting close. I could feel it.

• • •

In all my moments of spiritual liberation, moments sculpted out of an ability to stand alone, if briefly, there was a dormant sorrow. The sadness, I know now, was guilt. I never was able to nurture anything, a friend or a relative, with consistency. As a result, I often spent my time hiding from the expectations I raised in others. I would be there one day for them, absent the next few months, if not years, without a call or a letter. I would give them the world one day, and then disappear, avoiding the phone, weighed down by the demands I'd created. The friendships I imagined and birthed were errors of my dreams. My friends were baffled.

Shortly before I left Syracuse, Rosa, my best friend, had told me: "I can't just be there for you every time you show up and pretend everything is just fine with you disappearing and not caring for me." Her mother had died and I had been nowhere to be seen for months.

I felt anger toward her, not guilt. It was new. I said: "I give what I can and when I can. I am inconsistent and unreliable and this is the friend you have in me. I am sorry I've misled and failed you. Maybe one day it will be different."

The loss of this friend was the beginning of many losses out of this new attitude: "I am what I am and that's all that I am." It was an attitude born of chronic exhaustion at my desperate acts to be loved. This exchange was the beginning of seeing how broken I was and not being fearful of what others might see.

I wasn't as loving and generous as I'd thought. For a long time, my self-absorbed need to be loved had not admitted the real existence of those around me. Their souls were so tangled up in my needs and my consciousness that they were like scenery; part of the landscape of my diverse and frantic feelings. There were memories from the past and from books I treasured that were more real than most of the living, speaking people sharing my days. I could so easily welcome them into my life and dismiss them because they did not exist. This discovery did not shame me, perhaps because I believed that everyone, at some point, experienced something similar.

A time came when I could feel nothing and bear it. My heart could be vacant, just a few longings but nothing life arresting. I could pack up a car and leave a town I'd lived in for almost two decades for an unknown cold island. I could sit still for long enough to allow for moments when the world and those in it felt like thinking entities, living souls, capable of suffering, happiness, falling ill, dying. I began to care, to take care. I kept appointments. I returned phone calls. I did not offer to give what I couldn't afford to give. There is no doubt: our capacity for caring is the mirror of our needs, our dreams.

On the day I finally left Syracuse, there was no sun. I drove through a late January snowstorm for two days straight determined to get there because life lay ahead of me. Once in a while the reality of my cervical test hit me with a pang of panic and nausea. Yet, that too felt part of the quest. Somehow I was going to take care of it the same way I was taking care of the whiteout I was driving through.

I woke up on January 31 in a new home, a new bed, and it was my own. The roof over my head was my own, as long as I could pay the rent. I had breakfast in my little kitchen overlooking Stonington Harbor. I was on a remote island off the coast of Maine. All around me was seafaring memorabilia. Order shone from the meticulous decorations, the matching drapes and furniture and rugs. For too long I had lived wrapped up in chaos.

At the docks, a morning mist wet the boats and the pilings. Close by, a porthole held my face in its foggy circle of glass. I felt summoned to be responsible for the life I was.

On February 8, 2003, twelve days after Dan and I parted ways in Bennington and only six days after having moved to Maine, I was in his small house on a bend of the road in a dusty town outside Denver listening to Dan read from Walt Whitman's "Song of the Open Road." We sat in bed, our legs crossed and facing each other.

He said: "Listen, Irene."

And he read:

Camerado, I give you my hand!
I give you my love more precious than money,
I give you myself before preaching or law;
Will you give me yourself? Will you come and travel with me?
Shall we stick by each other as long as we live?

"Shall we?" he asked.

"I'm sorry, what?"

"Will you marry me?"

I felt like I was standing on a precipice, unsure if it was life or death I was looking at. I had just moved to Maine, ready to start a life on my own. So much had happened to get me there. Was I, after all, that afraid that my heart needed to pull this trick on me? Or was it that physically leaving Syracuse was half the battle and a big enough of a step to dare catching this curve ball life was throwing at me now?

I took the leap of faith. We married on March 6, after having been merely fifteen days in each other's company. The next two months were spent planning our church wedding in Puerto Rico. My two uncles were to officiate the ceremony at the Episcopalian cathedral my uncle Miguel headed. All my eighteen cousins were to be best women and men. I was to see my family, the Vilars and the Lebróns, gathered for the first time since my mother's death, twenty-five years earlier.

I arrived in Puerto Rico on May 15, 2003, in a state of euphoria and almost wounding expectation for the family reunion and reconciliation that my marriage was bringing about. I had a dream one night from which I woke up feeling like a stranger to myself. In the dream I was pregnant and inside of me were my baby and myself—another me. We were warm. But my mother's body, which was also my own, began growing cold. I wanted out. The hands that pulled at me were my own.

I began to feel anxious and restless. My thoughts grew disorganized. I told myself I was simply exhausted. I visited my grandmother Lolita, whom I had not spoken with since 1994. Back then I had called her to discuss my manuscript. My letters had gone unanswered. The book was not turning out to be the political manifesto she envisioned or the Evita-like Lolita Lebrón biography I'd once believed I wanted to write. My mother's life kept sneaking into the text and so did my own. I wanted and needed her to read the book and tell me what she thought.

I called her. "How are you Lolita?" I asked, clumsily.

Silence.

"Did you get my letters?"

"Why are you calling this house?" Her voice frightened me.

"But Lolita, I'm your granddaughter, I'm your family."

A loud, snorting laugh broke on the other end of the phone.

"Listen carefully, my family is the nation of Puerto Rico to which I have given my life and anyone, you listen well, anyone who threatens the nation is the enemy. I have fought for this nation and in the name of all the fallen ones in the struggle. Your mother is a fallen one. You are defiling her memory."

"Am I your enemy?"

"That book of yours, saying Tatita did not die in a car accident but killed herself, is a farce, and the nationalist movement won't take it. You publish that book and the movement won't forgive you."

"What about you, Lolita?"

"I am the Movement!"

I had hung up on that disembodied voice. Grandmother Lolita, the only bridge I had imagined between my mother and me, was merely one more projection of my feeble desires.

The image of the heroine rising from the dead, feeding off the thousands of casualties from the cause she'd lived for, was frightening and alien. I saw myself as just one woman holding on to the pathetic corpse of her mother, the only claimable casualty of my private struggle. My corpse against those of Lolita did not stand a chance in this absurd battle of the dead.

At her home, I felt her tentative embrace, heard her say that as long as there was no mention of that unfortunate book of mine, all would be fine. She appreciated my letter of reconciliation asking for the honor of having her give the toast at my wedding. She would. I left her home with a mixed feeling of gratitude and humiliation.

At the wedding reception, as Lolita walked up to the podium, I asked myself why I needed this stranger to sanction my life.

"You all gathered here know the sacrifices that go to the struggle of freeing a nation," Lolita said. "Friends and families," she continued, looking toward my table, "the close relatives of revolutionaries most of all, suffer a great deal."

Dan, at my side, tightened his grip on my hand.

"My family paid a big price. My son died. My daughter died. My granddaughter, Irene, lost her mother. Irene had a difficult life, suffered much. I wish it could have been different."

The champagne glass in Lolita's hand shook considerably. Her generous bright white hair reached the collar of her dress and framed her petite face with bangs that she had to keep moving off her eyes as the shaking worsened. At eighty-five, a recent bout with breast cancer and the onset of Parkinson's was gnawing away at her. Her convictions, too, were growing weak. There had never been acknowledgment of the costs of public mythmaking on her loved ones.

"But listen you all gathered here, in this happiest of occasions, let us all stand up and toast for my granddaughter's future." She raised her glass high above her head and some of the champagne spilled over her hair and the podium.

"Yes, let us all celebrate, let us raise our glasses, because Irene, today, has finally dried up her tears!"

Lolita held a trembling hand out to me, but I, in tears, only wanted her to stop talking.

I don't remember much of what she said next, which went on for a while. Dan asked if I was all right, and Dorothy, his mother, came over and sat next to me while I sobbed on her shoulder. When Dan took me by the hand and walked me over to Lolita at the end of the toast, I watched her drink from her flute while most of the champagne fell down the sides of her mouth and onto her dress. I wanted to run away.

It was similar to what I'd felt at my mother's funeral, when the woman with the rosary wrapped around the hand she waved at the crowds commanded, at the top of her lungs, for no one to shed a tear. High up in my father's arms, I could see people covering the entire grounds of the cemetery and beyond the fence. They were pushing dangerously at us standing by the pit. I was excited. But then the woman with the rosary, who had been introduced to me as my grandmother a few hours earlier, began to talk about my mother. No one should cry, the woman's voice kept repeating, because Gladys Myrna was not dead. Such was the case with all heroes of the motherland. I grew restless in my father's arms and he set me down. I wanted to run away but I was trapped. Above me, all the hands in the world clapped at a burning sun.

Soon after the wedding toast, sadness tinged with panic set in. It began while a picture was being taken of me with Claudia, my cousin's two-year-old girl, in my arms. We were staring straight into a large photographic lens while my cousin gave instructions to the photographer. A picture swam across my vision, bringing back memories of my brother's wedding when I last saw my mother. In that photograph, Claudia's mother was in my mother's arms, their cheeks pressed against each other, their eyes and smiles fastened to the camera. My heart pounded. In the seconds before the flash, my life suddenly seemed only as real as my ravaged cervix. I would never bear a child. I could never undo what I had done. And Lolita, she and I could never undo what had taken place, in spite of her toast.

At the age of eight I walked two miles to the cemetery to bury my mother and I cracked jokes for every weeping aunt on the way there. I went on to get straight *A*s in seven schools in seven years and entered college at fifteen. Soon after, I moved in with a man thirty-four years my senior and remained with him for a decade. I always thought I'd be somebody. I have imagined myself a president, a saint, mother, sailor, writer, publisher, mother again. Many times over I imagined myself a mother.

What I never imagined was me at thirty-four sitting next to my husband on an airplane headed to Europe for an overdue honeymoon, asking myself how I could ever be a mother to the child in my womb. I should have felt like the luckiest woman on earth. I was pregnant and a follow-up cervical test had been negative. I wasn't depressed. I knew too well how that felt. But a pervasive sadness was nesting in me, the feeling that something was going cockeyed with my life. It had started on my trip home for the wedding and deepened at the news of my pregnancy.

For six months, I had turned our bathroom into a fertility lab crowded with ovulation predictor kits, thermometers of all kinds, conception books, and cycle charts. When I got my period in August after being a week late, I sat on the toilet feeling hopeless. I would never be able to have a child. I knew it, the same way I knew with crushing clarity that I was a woman with fifteen abortions under her cervix. I got pregnant the month I gave up any hope of conceiving.

Sometime in December I found out I was carrying a girl. The image on the screen was clear. The doctor traced the curve of her vertebral column and what he said was a leg and pointed at the perfectly visible toes. I taped the ultrasound picture on my bathroom mirror. Whenever I went to the bathroom, I stopped and stared at the black and white ultrasound film with the three pictures. In one the head and trunk of the fetus curled around a hand stretched wide open. I could count five fingers. In another the head was turned a little toward me. The last image was of one big toe cupped in a baby's hand.

One night when I couldn't fall asleep, the idea came of putting family pictures into an album. The pictures had lain in a box for almost a year. I opened the box and there was the picture of my mother pregnant with me mixed in with our wedding proofs. I framed it and hung it in the nursery. I stood in the middle of the empty room, looking at this woman for clues to the mother I was to become. We could have had a relationship, I thought. She could be soothing me now, telling me everything would be fine. I took the picture off the wall.

I needed to gather myself, to make sense of my life, which went on while I remained outside of it. I felt I did the same things every day, thought the same thoughts, cooked, ate, read, yet I was different. In the supermarket there were other women, with their empty bellies, and there was me. In my family in Denver, there were my sisters-in-law with their mothers at their sides, and there was me.

I sat on the floor of the nursery and read the chapter of my own book about my mother's death. Then I flipped back to the sections of our times together. In one scene she comes into my room where I'm lying in bed, kneels before me, and asks if I will still love her when she's gone. On the book's original paperback cover, she sits on a rock by a beach, she's turned sideways out to sea. I'm sitting beside her. A rush of connection stung me, an interweaving of emotion and memory. But just as this awareness came over me, it was gone, and the woman and the child were again a picture on a book cover.

I drifted off to sleep. When I woke with a start, I was angry. It was a new, foreign feeling. I was angry with my mother, finally.

In the days to come I found myself thinking hard about her. I began to think about my past pregnancies. I began to think about the pang in my stomach seeing my baby move in the ultrasound; the four chambers of her heart pulsating. I began to be aware of the relationship I'd set in motion. I realized that for years I had wrestled, without knowing, with whether a relationship should continue to develop between myself as mother, and a fetus as child, and between myself and my body, my history and my future.

As I looked back, I couldn't see much thought but carelessness, my looking the other way, the trance-like life I led. I had changed. I heard myself more. For most of my life, I heard others far more clearly than I did myself. This could sum up my life. The things I put up with for love. I told myself I needed to be closer to Dan's mother. I needed the wisdom and perspective from a mother who watched her children grow.

In our new home in Evergreen, Colorado, I stood at the kitchen sink washing dishes with the sounds of my husband's children in the background; twelve-year-old Bella's silence hovering in my ears and seven-year-old Nathanael's longing for his birth mom, tugging at my paralysis. Dan's movements about the room taking care of everything were a reminder of my ineptness. The food I was cooking was a crushing warning of thousands of suppers to come.

I went to the bathroom and stared in the mirror. The woman it gave back to me was as tired as she'd ever been. I wished for a hole to crawl into. It all felt infested with dread, the evening, my lovely mountain home, the air we all breathed.

I closed my eyes and prayed for clarity, but my prayer only turned into a flood of memories: I am eight years old and then ten and twelve and fifteen and eighteen and in a cemetery and in a classroom and kneeling down by the bedside in a convent school, and roaming the subway in Mexico City, and sailing across the Gulf Stream, a few times I see this crossing, back and forth, and I am aground off St. Augustine by a green buoy I can touch with my right hand and I am curled up naked in a bunk bed in the aft cabin of a sailboat trying to write, wiping off my sweat from the keyboard with my panties until he knocks at the door saying his work day is over and he's hungry. I hear him knocking year after year and I am seventeen and nineteen and twenty-two and twenty-five and twenty-nine, and I am burning my hands as I change injectors and bleed an engine while the boat heels until the deck fasteners are below my eye level and I pray, already then with the prayers, I pray that I bleed the goddamn thing before he comes down and sends me up on deck to grab the helm.

I saw twenty-five years wrapped up in one single, repetitive action that is more like a reaction, the effort made around others whose love I had to gain. I saw myself in many kitchens washing dishes, frantic to please my hostess, an aunt, a friend's mother, a teacher, a nun, a girlfriend, a boyfriend, my ex-husband's friends, and making up beds that are not my bed, and opening medicine cabinets and staring at their contents, wishing for the day I'd have my own things.

I saw the past four years of my semi-single life, even if I had lived with another wrong man for part of it. I saw the good job, the graduate education, the travels and the people and the power and the woman in me finally finding her way. I saw the lonely days when I at last packed up the car and left the city I'd lived in for over half my life and in it, the two wrong men. I wondered if I could be happy with this mother I had fashioned for myself overnight.

So we talked, Dan and I, and he asked about my happiness.

"You can tell me everything, let me help you."

"I can't be a mother. I can't do it. I want to abort." I couldn't believe I said it, but I had. I wanted to abort the child I had begged God for for over seven months. I felt I was going insane.

What was wrong with me? I had a family I loved; I had two stepchildren who called me Mom and took on my Spanish accent out of empathy for the mother I was and out of longing for the mother I was not. I'd found a man whose love had climbed up the length of my spine, straightening it. The air he breathed into me had flared open my senses. I saw, I felt, I tasted, and what's more, I heard. I heard so much more. And yet, I was sad.

He took my head between his hands. "Of course," he kissed my forehead, "all your body knows is how unkind you've been to yourself. It must be strange, perhaps even scary, Irene, to be kind to yourself." He hugged me tight.

"The truth is you will be a ferociously loving mother pouring all your boundless love where it will thrive for real."

I hugged Dan back for dear life. He stepped back and looked long into my eyes with that smile of his that reminded me of one's viable trust in life's infinite resources.

As we hugged, I wished our love would survive us both.

At around the same time, when I was feeling the most doubtful about the pregnancy, I dreamt about my father. There was a field of cilantro, giant blades of cilantro, and father was between them, trapped against the bulb-like roots of the greens. He was not upset. It looked like he was at home there. As for me, it was a pleasant sight, all that cilantro. I was looking up from somewhere close to the ground and could see strands of blue sky and rushing clouds. Then the left side of the dream caught on fire. It broke out in between the roots and moved up the stalks so fast I barely had time to catch my father's surprised look as he turned toward me, concerned, and a pungent, spicy smell of freshly washed cilantro filled my lungs and forced my eyes shut.

I woke up shaken by the realization that my father was growing old and weak. I called him.

"What's up, Dumbo?" he sang into the phone.

"I dreamt you were stuck in the middle of a cilantro field when it caught on fire. I woke up just as the blazing flames were reaching you. I was scared for you and yet the cilantro smelled good."

"Wasn't that your chore every day after school, to go fetching cilantro for your mother's cooking?" I'd forgotten.

"You had to find it in between the weeds and then wash stem by stem in case the dogs had pissed on it. You were always late getting back to the kitchen. Your mother had to go looking for you. She often found you feeding the cilantro to the land crabs."

"I miss you Dad."

"I miss you too, Dumbo."

"How are you?"

"What kind of question is that? You know I'm an old horse with lots of grass still around to munch on." Dad whinnied like the animal he loved. "But how is my new mother-to-be loving daughter?"

"I'm scared. I love Dan and I'm unhappy. I don't think I can be a mother." There, I've said it. What was he going to do? We had no practice at reaching out to each other.

"I doubt what I'm going to tell you will help you Dumbo, but it might because once it helped me. We expect life to be pleasant and find all the discomforts in it surprising, as if we've been wronged, when it is the other way around. Life sucks, Dumbo."

"What am I to do?"

"For six weeks after your mother died, I didn't leave my bed. Your uncle Cheo kicked some sense into me. I was thirty-seven years old and he called me a child. He told me it was time to grow up. 'Go on, waste away,' he called from the door, 'or come out here and check out your daughter. She's way up in a tree. So I got out of bed to check on you.

"Don't go wasting away your life on a soap opera, Dumbo. It is a good thing for your dream to have caught on fire. You have your own family. You are making your own home. Enough with the past. Irene, I tell you now, it's time to grow up. Go check on your husband and eat well."

Shortly after New Year's, looking out of my kitchen window at Mount Evans in the distance, I could feel Miguel and Fonso looking out of my eyes. We were home. Once, not long before, any view from a window showed a world where we were alien.

· In the evening, after eight months away from it, I took up writing again. It happened like this, in an uneventful, quiet way. I wrote:

How can I give testimony to the horror I precipitated upon a girl fifteen different times? Yes, I am an abortion addict and I do not wish for a scapegoat. Everything can be explained, justified, our last century tells us. Everything may be except for the burden of life interrupted that shall die with me.

As I wrote the words down, I felt delivered from a damned life and I imagined, at last, the face of my daughter.

My mother was a Valium addict and my father was addicted to alcohol and gambling. Two of my brothers were heroin addicts. If my body was my perspective on the world, then it was a battleground of hopefulness and hopelessness, and fear, just like my brothers'.

As early as that summer of my twelfth birthday when my father remarried, I suffered from loss of sleep, headaches, stomach problems, lack of appetite, weight loss, inability to focus, isolation. I excelled in school and set out to skip another grade. I went to Haiti twice with my teacher nuns and became obsessed with their missionary work. I turned toward my grandmother Lolita and fantasized of becoming a diplomatic version of her. I took on my new little sisters Diana and Miri as my own children.

When I met the man who became my master, I had been an overachiever, having dealt with my terrors and low self-esteem through total immersion in the acts and aid of others. And I had fallen prey to their wishes. I lived up to expectations in order to not lose protection and love. I easily embedded myself in the powers of others. As for him, his powers were my weaknesses, his truths my lies, his courage to be free was my cowardice as a woman.

As a fifteen-year-old college freshman, seven years after my mother's death, buying books on adoption in the Syracuse University bookstore, I was finding refuge in fantasies of mothering.

In the face of paralysis, my maternal desire surfaced to ward off any awareness of distress. Those first college months are the first recollection I have of actively avoiding the void before me with mothering, imparting my capacity to mother with power and agency. I was also fashioning that capacity as both avoidance and face-off, as flight and as return. I would only need to become sexually active and have an abortion within the year for my body to get a taste of the drama of life and death it would come to crave.

My story is a perversion of both maternal desire and abortion, framed by a lawful procedure that I abused. My first pregnancy was a result of lying about birth control. He was inside of me when he asked: You are protecting yourself, aren't you? Later, I would take my pills and skip a day, a few, and often give up on the whole month, promising myself I would do better the next time. Not knowing how a pill or a handful of them would affect my fertility, my days took on a balancing act, and a high of sorts accompanied the days before my period was due. Half my pregnancies with him occurred during our first three years together. Each time I got my period, I was sad. Each time I discovered I was pregnant, I was aroused and afraid. Every pregnancy was a house of mirrors I entered and lost myself in, numb to the realities of a fetus, my partner's wishes, and the impossible motherhood I was fashioning.

I never craved that moment when I clenched my vibrating abdomen, feet high up on cold stirrups, and told myself never again. There was no high that came with that. My mood-altering experience was a shape shifter. At times the high took place before pregnancy, waiting for a missed period, my body basking in the promise of being in control. At other times it was the pregnancy itself, the control I embodied if only for a couple of months, and still other times it was leaving the abortion clinic, feeling that once again I had succeeded in a narrow escape. The time of my drama was my time, no one could interrupt it, and what was more important, I could not interrupt it to meet others' needs.

Feelings of inadequacy, helplessness, and disorder faded in the face of the possibilities of my reproductive body. An excitement, hyperarousal, almost euphoria surrounded my maternal desire. The craving gave structure to the confusing morass of events that made up my life. I would visit Marshall's and put infant clothes on lay-away. I would start a diary. I would daydream about holding a baby girl and teaching her the alphabet. I would lie in the bathtub with a smile on my face, knowing that only I knew.

Tension would gradually build as my pregnant body crowded out all other things and emotions. After a few weeks, stress would set in and grow more acute by the day and with the physical changes in me. I would go in and out of denial. At times I would forget I was pregnant. Other times I could think of nothing else. I would stop eating. By the time I lay in an abortion clinic waiting for the procedure to begin, I would feel nothing but disgust and shame. When I left the clinic, I felt a calm respite, surrender. I always said to myself then, "This has to end."

It was a violent, intensely emotional drama that kept me from feeling alone. A moment came when not being pregnant was enough motivation for wanting to be pregnant. The fantasies subsided. Soon it was no longer about the control I had craved before. Getting pregnant began to be simply a habit. If I wasn't pregnant, something was wrong, more wrong than what was already wrong. I believe this habit formed with abortion #9 and pregnancy #10, shortly after I returned from Miguel's funeral. I didn't want anything to do with my husband or the pregnancy or myself. I overdosed and woke up in a hospital. I needed another self-injury to get the high.

• • •

I can't think about my mother and in general Puerto Rican women without thinking about "choice." The language of choice invokes free will based on individual freedom, obscuring the dynamics between social constraints and human activity. Choices are framed by larger institutional structures and ideological messages. While population growth has been blamed for Puerto Rico's widespread poverty, other causes, such as American exploitation, were ignored or covered up. The 1967 NBA winner for nonfiction, *La Vida* by Oscar Lewis, reiterated the views of U.S. social scientists in turning fertility and reproduction into the source of the "Puerto Rican problem." The Puerto Rican mother was either victimized by her macho husband and countless children, longing to be rescued from her own ignorance, or a relentless dangerous mating machine that needed to be stopped.

Throughout my mother's childbearing years, from 1955 to 1969, Puerto Rico was a human laboratory for the development of birth control technology and population control policies. Pills twenty times stronger than those used today, with dangerous systemic side effects, including sterility, were tested on women by the U.S. government, which was simultaneously studying the long-term effects of secondary syphilis on a group of African-American men in Tuskegee without treating them for the disease. In 1968, women in Puerto Rico were more than ten times more likely to be sterilized than were women in the United States. By 1974, 37 percent of Puerto Rican women of childbearing age had been permanently sterilized. In my small town of Barceloneta, 25,000 women were sterilized between 1955 and 1975. By 1980, Puerto Rico had the highest per-capita rate of sterilization in the world.

My mother was sixteen when she gave birth to Fonso in January 1956. In April, she became pregnant with Cheo and gave birth in October to a six-month preemie. Shortly after that, she began using Enovid, the controversial 10-milligram birth control pill. In September 1961, after the birth of my brother Miguel, the public hospital staff threatened not to provide care if she did not consent to a tubal ligation. Eight years later, my mother's tied tubes became untied and I was conceived. In 1974, when a pap smear showed nonmalignant, abnormal cell growth, the doctor recommended a hysterectomy. My mother was sent home without a reproductive system and no hormonal treatment. She was thirty-three years old.

Most of the conscious memories I have of my mother belong to the time after her hysterectomy. Depression and mood swings fastening her to a chair or sending her away in the middle of the night. Migraines curled her blood-clotted body in bed. Irritability slapped a daughter for asking a question. Bloating and fat gain in the hips and thighs shamed her in the mirror.

What growing up poor and an orphan, the daughter of a woman imprisoned in the United States and being the wife for twenty-three years of a man unable to value her could not do, the U.S. mass-sterilization program and its racist population-control ideologies did. Self medicating with Valium and acting out a ransacked, frantic, if vacant, sexuality, my mother came undone while I watched.

The solutions my grandmother and my mother crafted for their impotence had Romanticism's (and Marx's) defiant phrase "I am nothing and should be everything" inherent in them. Both strived in their own ways for larger realities that would give them self-validation. I couldn't stand alone and reached out for support in motherhood. After all, I grew up in a family informed by the romantic narrative of Albizu Campos: "the brazenness of the Yankee invaders has reached the extremes of trying to profane Puerto Rican mother-hood; of trying to invade the very insides of nationality."

I used to believe that I was a happy child who had the misfor-tune of watching a mother die. The repeat abortions were symp-toms of recklessness and low self-esteem, at times related to depressive states. I was as numb toward them as I was toward my mother's suicide. Only when I shocked myself by saying "I am an abortion addict" was I forced to think of myself as a trauma victim. Trauma is an affliction of the powerless, telling us that we are unable to affect the outcome of our own lives. Sudden, uncontrollable be-havior is an essential part of the development of post-traumatic stress.

When my mother opened the door of the small Mazda my fa-ther was driving on our way home from my brother Cheo's wed-ding, I called out "Mami!" and I remember the hard pull of her shoulder in my hand as I reached out. But abandonment began much earlier than her death. There are fragmented memories of waiting alone in deserted parking lots, beaches, smelly hallways of motels, my own bedroom. In all these memories, I'm waiting for my mother to come back.

I had no control over my mother's decision to abandon me. But I had control over my body. I could impregnate myself and abort; no one else could control my fate when I showed such strange ownership. Repeat abortions "remembered" an element of the experience of death and abandonment. If my mother chose death over me, I chose to tell the story fifteen terrifying times.

What was I to do? After all, my mother was a gothic character who jumped out of a car to her death. Her mother was a very romantic one, going into the U.S. Congress with a gun in her purse and shooting at everybody there. For some reason, I'm not as ambitious. I chose a more intimate theater to play out my drama. My grandmother burst out in boundless megalomania, transcending all limits. My mother bogged down into wormwood like a worthless sinner. My drama had a longing for protection at its center. My parents' inability to protect me is a result of the melodrama men and women act out in our culture. This 24/7 soap opera is addictive in itself, and so they, obliged to tune in full time, had little left for their offspring. In their soap opera, my father was the master at mixed messages. He valued his wives while devaluing them. Both women were addicts. My mother to Valium and my stepmother to inhaling Real Kill bug spray. My father's message to them was: I love you and for your own good I must leave you. In both marriages my father came out looking good while the women seemed out of control.

Self-mutilation, an inability to self-protect, is a common response to abandonment. There are as many theories for self-injury as there are trauma survivors—escaping feelings of emptiness, easing tension, expressing pain, punishing the body as a way of expressing responsibility for the "abuse," providing a sense of control and mastery. My repetition compulsion was based on impulsive acts to ward off experiencing aloneness and badness. Dissociation was an opportunity for magical thinking, a sense of mastery to overcome my powerlessness, hopelessness, and learned helplessness. As I now understand it, my drama looked like this: tension gradually builds (pregnancy), the painful battering incident occurs (abortion), a calm respite follows. Arousal before the violence and the peace of surrender afterward both reinforce the traumatic bond between victim and abuser.

The role I took on in mothering my dying dog of fifteen years, Oliveira, was crucial in breaking the cycle. Oliveira was powerless, my child self and my imaginary, impossible fetus/baby. My mother was neglectful, my adult self. When I found him half dead in the kennel, I had become the abuser, the neglecter. My deep anger at my abandonment, at death, at helplessness came out and I hit rock bottom. Total defacement. The dissociation I'd lived, internalizing my mother's neglect and self-destruction as part of my self, was revealed. And with this, the continuing role of my past traumatic experience on my current life was shaken and realigned.

I have been called a survivor, but truly I wasn't one. I was a deluded creature in suspended animation. Survival is a phenomenon of consciousness, a discovery of oneself as a tenacious entity. I was not a survivor until I overcame my fear of mothering the child in my womb. It was halfway through my sixteenth pregnancy that I found peace with my maternal desire and fell in love with my situation and the future gestating in me. My daughter Loretta Mae became the coherence emerging from the shameful mass of thirty-five years.

On one side of my bathroom mirror there are several pictures of my daughter Loretta Mae. In one, she is inside an incubator, a few minutes old, turned sideways toward the camera, eyes wide open, left hand stretched out on her cheek. In a second, she is sitting with my help on a picnic table staring out at the sea. In a third, both she and I are asleep and her little three-month-old head is nestled in the crook of my arm. Through all the changes that these pictures preserve, my daughter remains the same little girl.

On the other side of my bathroom mirror I keep a picture of Loretta taken December 22, 2003, eighteen weeks before she was born. The ultrasound images show clearly a miniature head tilted back, an arm raised up, with the hand pointing back toward the face. It would have been possible and permissible to end her life at this point.

EPILOGUE

MARCH 1, MONDAY · I'm lying in the hammock Dan hung for me in the backyard between two ponderosa pines. It is an unusually warm day for March. Dusk is arriving low, and it seems not to fall over things but to come from inside them. I prefer dusk in Puerto Rico, falling suddenly and fast, like a curtain coming down on a stage.

But there is an aloof tranquility, peace, to what surrounds me in my hammock. I wonder if it is because nature, and especially this foreign nature, doesn't know me. I've grown close, intimate, with these parts of my life in America in ways I have not and don't believe I will ever be with Puerto Rico. Mount Evans, for example, has become mine. It's roaring tundra, the snow, the wild goats roaming its rocks, the thousand-year-old bristlecone pines, the anonymous, ancient dirt of the ground, its faceless, sphinx-like glacier. All of it, nestled in the constant wind at fourteen thousand feet, is her unawareness of me, and its presence, towering over this home, soothes and lulls me, and maybe because its voice isn't human. I've lived periods of respite in this country mainly in the presence of nature. In these moments I've forgotten all of my life's mistakes and desires. I've grown tender with compassion toward myself and everything else.

It happened at boarding school while tapping maple trees in a

New Hampshire forest when I was ten, and in upstate New York swimming Adirondack secluded lakes a few times in my teens, and often during that first boat trip down the Intracoastal Waterway the summer I turned nineteen. Sailing into Cape May a flock of geese flew so low and close to the boat that a wing got in my mouth. I can still hear the geese's call as they parted ways to dodge the sails and formed again in the distance. In Beaufort, North Carolina, wild ponies ran along a beach to starboard as I entered the channel, their necks turned toward the boat and their hoofs splashing the water. In St. Augustine two manatees played backflips around the anchor rope stopping sometimes to sing to me for another leaf of lettuce. In Ft. Lauderdale a total eclipse followed me into the harbor one midnight under sail. The engine had died some miles offshore and a fading moon led me in to disappear altogether the minute I dropped the anchor.

There is something freeing whenever nature and I have met. In each encounter, beginning with the "pastoral" life in Boynton School, I've felt touched by a sort of purposefulness, so pleasant to be a part of, and so foreign to my own troubles. I wonder what and how this will change when I give birth and my eyes meet my daughter's.

Right now, being pregnant feels much like such encounters with nature. This morning my belly button popped out and I noticed for the first time a dark line underneath running down and disappearing under my pubic hair. I'm entering my seventh month and most of my interests have narrowed and turned inward. I am concerned only with the little female human being who will be born. I suspect this little girl will be mine in the deepest possible sense, and I will be hers. I catch myself wondering what she already knows about me.

• • •

MARCH 26, FRIDAY • At the State University of New York
I gave a lecture today on the writing of memoirs and read about
abortion with a round, big pregnant belly keeping me far from
the microphone. I didn't think I could do it. As I walked to the
podium I kept saying to myself: They won't understand. You'll
be despised. I began writing a memoir on abortion in order to
think out my own particular choices, my own individual selves
and the fate they'd fashioned. I had the feeling that my experience was very different from other people's. But one older man,
in his sixties, came to me as I was leaving the auditorium. He
introduced himself as a professor at the college. He said that he
believed in Bergson's and Thomas Davidson's speculations of the
existence of a vital ontology of organismic self-feeling. All beings, he said in a strong British accent, were attracted to beauty,
goodness, and perfection. Kant found this inner sensitivity something like a conscience, "the moral law within man," he quoted.
The heart of nature had this self-expansion beat. The difference
was that we humans were the only organism fated to puzzle out
what it meant to feel right and thus lived with an excruciating
paradox of urges. On one hand, we desire to merge with the rest
of nature, to disappear into something larger in an attempt to
escape standing alone, impotent, in the face of nature and inevitable death. On the other hand, we want to be unique, to stand
out, apart from everything. Knowing this, he said, could any
teenager—like his seventeen-year-old daughter, who got pregnant, wanted the child, then aborted and committed suicide three
days later—have any chance at life if she herself was the battlefield
of such a splitting paradox? I wish I'd had something meaningful to say to him at that moment. But it is clear to me now that

we all yearn to inform our fates, to evolve another life pattern, more genuine, and less drawn by fear.

APRIL 19, MONDAY • Today is our third day on Isla Mujeres. Finally Dan and I begin to relax in the small confines of this Mexican palapa by the ocean. It took us a few days to get used to the guano raining down on the mosquito net covering our bed. The caretaker told us it was just the lizards living in the palapa roof. Every palapa had them and God bless those lizards, she said, because they kept the bugs away. It reminds me of my childhood, this simple, earthy home where there is not much separating outdoors from indoors. At night my mother used to put a bowl of water beneath each of the bed legs to stop the centipedes and fire ants from crawling up while I slept. My brother Miguel and I used to bet candy on the number of bugs in the bowl. He always won. This morning, as Dan slept, I found a baby lizard on his back. I watched them, thinking of the life we are searching for, the reason why we came down to this island. We both want a simpler day, a place to raise our children without highways and cars splitting our family and thoughts. Clearly, this island will not work. Too many retirees and few children, unless we live in town in the midst of a frantic tourism or in the outskirts where third-world poverty stares you down. We'll have to keep looking elsewhere but meanwhile we are getting the vacation we so much needed before the baby arrives.

I felt almost depressed the first few days, almost as if my tired body and tired mind took over completely and a strange apathy was all I could feel toward this island heaven. But today begins to feel differently. I should have remembered that about living by the sea, in a small island far from the entanglements of city or suburbia. The first days are always like that, just like when first arriving on *Sarabande* each winter; I'm forced against a radically different rhythm and I have to shed the person I am on arriving, give way to a slowed-down self. Then, at some point, the mind begins to awaken just as I begin to grow accustomed to getting along with very little. Less clothing, less shelter; no airtight shelter of the North here but a bare palapa of lizards. My hair is graying. I'm letting it do what it wants.

This morning, while Dan slept with his lizard, I walked along the beach, feeling that this pregnancy has given me the gift of solitude, the capacity and need to be alone in order to find again the inner stillness I felt as a child in the woods of a New Hampshire boarding school wanting to be a saint and again while living on a boat and dreaming of sailing around the world. Carrying my daughter is teaching me that everything in my life, until now, has been a distraction.

MAY 1, SATURDAY · I went to the midwife this morning afraid I had ruptured my membranes and would go into labor seven weeks early. She took a pH test of the fluid leaking out of me and assured me it was not amniotic fluid. But I am not at peace. I took a nap this afternoon and the leaking worsened. The fluid pours out when I'm lying down and stops somewhat when I walk. I called the midwife again and she told me I had the option to go to the hospital but that they would simply play the liability game and put me on heavy doses of antibiotics. If I wanted to give birth at home, I needed to follow her advice. Yet, I have the gut feeling I am going to deliver this baby prematurely. I don't care if she tells me there is no cervical effacement present. I can't sleep thinking of how all the abortions might be threatening the life of my daughter.

When my midwife first saw me early in the pregnancy I was afraid she would ask about my past pregnancies. When she did, she did not seem surprised. She looked up from her notebook and told me it was okay, a woman's body was stronger than it seemed. Then she examined me. My legs spread, socks on, her fingers in, hands pushing down on my belly. She asked if I wanted to see my cervix. She inserted a speculum, opened it wide and placed a mirror at the entrance, facing me. I had no scar tissue whatsoever, she said. I would definitely deliver to term. I remember holding back the tears and saying to myself, who is this woman, God bless her. A gesture of kindness and reassurance from a stranger is heartbreaking.

Now, nothing she says can convince me there isn't anything wrong. But I so much want to have my baby in my own bed. If only my cervix could hold on until the thirty-seventh week. If I go into labor before then the midwife can't deliver Loretta Mae at home.

MAY 5, WEDNESDAY • Loretta Mae was born this morning at 10:07, five pounds, twelve ounces and nineteen and a half inches long. She was six weeks early. I can see her lying in the middle of her incubator with her eyes closed and her tiny chest heaving up and down like a bird's. I held her the moment she was born, before the nurses rushed her to the intensive care unit. It was something I had imagined many times; she cradled in my arms, everything in place, the nursery back home waiting. An hour ago I held her in my arms again, tried to nurse her for the first time. She latched on but quickly fell asleep. I was unable to be at ease with my own daughter in my arms. She's so small, so fragile. The nurses seemed more at ease, handling her tiny body.

After I put her back in the glass box, I looked around the unit at other incubators, other tiny beings, tinier than mine, most of them on oxygen, and their lungs working too hard. I realized that as difficult as it was to watch others do the caregiving, I was grateful that my daughter had been born healthy. Right then I let it all go and sat down with my baby again. I rocked her naked body against my bare chest until I understood she was born.

Another mom nursing her preemie asked me earlier what birth was like for me. Now that I've held my baby I know that birth, for me, is keeping her alive. The milk must come, I've got to pump, I have to rock her naked body against my bare chest all night, I must keep her warm, her temperature stable. My Loretta must live.

JUNE 23, THURSDAY • Father has came to see us. At the airport I find him in a wheelchair in a corner of the baggage claim area. My brother Cheo is arguing with him. Father will not drink the water my brother had given him. They both complain to me at the same time. My brother is a pest, my father stubborn like an old, crabby bull. I am grateful they have each other.

He had almost died two weeks earlier from bleeding varicose veins in his stomach. The hemorrhage was a result of an alcoholism he supposedly had no idea about. He drank every night while he worked at his office, had never missed a day's work, he said. He recovered, was put on medication to help his damaged liver, but on the plane, he fainted and a pain so severe he can't walk settled in his lower abdomen. I have to take him to the emergency room straight from the airport.

"No more moonshine for me," he says with a smile.

At the emergency room, I notice his sunken features. He is in a half-sitting position, propped up by pillows; his shoulders are bare under the hospital gown and the skin hangs from the bone as if his is an old man's body. I feel my stomach turn and I look away. My father's feet and ankles are outside the bedclothes. Hairs have fallen off his calves and the skin has taken on a translucent shine covered with brown age spots. The left ankle is swollen and is considerably darker than the other. I put my hand on it and am shocked to realize I do so to cover it from my sight more than anything else.

"Those are the hooves of a bull," Father says. "And that one is the miracle one I almost lost to a motorcycle when I wanted to die in those hellish months after your mother was gone."

He laughs swiftly and rubs the back of my neck. His brown-green eyes gleam from his yellow skin; tender wide wrinkles mark their edges, his mouth turns up slightly.

"Dad, you have to take care of yourself," I say with a smile because with my father, everything has to be done with a smile. Nothing could ever be too wrong to merit forgetting we came from nothing and are to end up as nothing. He is as much a priest as his two ordained brothers, no matter what a son of a bitch he is.

Later, after the doctor has come in and said my father's cirrhosis is not only advanced but aggravated by alcohol-induced diabetes, I understand my father is going to die. Not that day or the next, but not in the distant future either. Shortly after the doctor leaves the room my father dozes off. I watch his features gradually relax, his chest rise and fall, realizing I have never watched my father sleep. I haven't looked at him much, either. What lives we lead that we don't notice our parents until moments like this, when death is pressed against our eyes.

The thought that they too have tried to find a way in life floods my heart with a great wave of respect and admiration.

• • •

JANUARY 28, 2005, TUESDAY • My body will never forget you. I go on sleeping on the futon by your crib even if you have stopped sleeping with me. It's been two months and each night I lie by your crib missing your tiny head on my shoulder, your warm, sweet breath on my chin. I looked forward to the time you would accept the crib, but I never expected the shift to be so painful. A few months ago you began waking up every hour, cranky and not wanting to nurse. I had to walk you back to sleep only for you to wake up within the hour. One night I counted nine wakings and three hours of walking. I knew you wanted the crib, that each one of my moves in bed disturbed you, my smell, my breath, my body, my weight. Now you are sleeping three-to-four hour stretches. I lie here next to you living the end of one special period in our relationship, wondering how many more there'll be, telling myself I must let you go, for our sake.

I know what despair is. I'm seeing it grow side by side with my love for you. I watch you grow by the hour, the day, each bath we take together every afternoon, the babble straining with meaning, and I am helpless in capturing the present, helpless in preventing it from turning into the past. I know part of the despair is my mother's loss anchored in the past, my separation from my father and home shortly after, and the inevitable death lurking in the future. I am a nostalgic who has long refused to mourn the loss of her objects by living off fusing with the wrong substitutes. But you, Loretta Mae, you are the right and meaningful substitute. Still, I catch myself squeezing an inch too hard when you want out of my arms as I am trying to rock or walk you to sleep. I feel a tightening in my chest when I witness your baby person wanting me only on your own terms as you crawl away. At times I surprise myself missing the baby infant of the first six months, sedentary and contemplative, needing me fully, on your terms as well, of course, but so close, so close to me.

MARCH 18, THURSDAY • Your aunt Julie just had her third daughter. In the hospital I reached out my arms for your cousin Emma and before even touching her I could feel the small, curling-into-you shape of the newborn, I could smell the baby scent, and tears flowed. It was a deep sorrow that cut through me, a mixture of memory and hope, of chances lost and inexorable fate. Emma was ten hours old. You were ten months. I was thirty-five. My mother sixty-four.

Most women I talk to begin to forgive their mothers and to love them more deeply when they themselves become mothers. They find themselves accepting the limitations of their mothers. Our case, Loretta, I'm afraid to say, is the opposite. My love for you has awakened anger toward your grandmother I never imagined I could feel. Looking into your eyes and losing my breath over the loving hold you've got on me, I can't fathom how my mother did not look into mine, did not allow me to hang on. I can understand intellectually all the reasons why a mother may find herself unable to mother. In a way, I've mothered my mother; I've given her the benefit of an idealized memory. It is not a special thing; this burden is common among neglected daughters. But I never felt anger over this role until you came. And I never before saw myself as neglected.

Last night we were bathing together. You were balancing on your little legs while holding onto my shoulders. Your fingernails dug deep into my skin, and it was painful but I let you go on. You were so happy. Suddenly, disturbing images reached out from the corners of a familiar, pleasant memory. Your grandmother was giving me a sponge bath with rose water before bedtime. She used to do that. I didn't want the sponge bath. I hate the smell of rose water. I suddenly sensed the rose water was rubbing alcohol. It stung my eyes. I hated the rough feel of the sponge. I was burning. I looked up at my mother, pleading, and she did not look at me but rubbed harder and dug her nails into my shoulder. I was sobbing, quietly, so as not to bother her. I understood she was upset. I understood giving me the bath annoyed her. It was her idea. I didn't need it. She needed it. But she was not happy.

So, Loretta Mae, what you will find in this story, when the time comes, is not so much the individual history of your mother but her relationship to the world cast by her origins. Your mother's truth, the most significant moments in her life, are not lodged in her memory, but haunt her and flee from her alternately. If I have, my love, learned something substantial that I wish you to know as early in life as possible, it is how slippery life is: how one evening I'm a six-year-old falling asleep holding on to my mother's soft wrist to wake up next a teen with a sail line burning through my hand; and how, when the thunderstorm passes and the Gulf Stream is blue again, I go below decks and come back up a thirty-five-year-old, cradling your newborn's tiny hands in my own.

JULY 6, MONDAY · I read books on psychology and infant development, searching for all the ways I can protect you from me. I'm haunted by visions of you at fifteen, alone in a foreign city feeling inadequate, unloved, staring at shop windows while sophisticated-looking women pass by. I don't want you to live the anguish of feeling trapped in the wrong body. I don't want you to ever succumb to the dismembered life of a false self. I don't want you ever to lie on a stretcher at an abortion clinic, your feet propped up on cold, steel stirrups. Your fate depends, a great deal, on me. Writing this down, in part, is my own fantasy of shielding you from my history.

SEPTEMBER 12, MONDAY • Man-O-War-Cay. A day with you. We wake in the same small room to the sound of wind through the palm trees and the sleep-breathing rhythms of waves on the shore. You are nursing and staring up at your hand waving good-bye to the curtain wafting above our heads. It's 6:05 AM. You sit up and applaud when you hear me say to you, "*Buenos Días*, Loretta." You beam a six-toothed smile at the window and point your index finger outside saying "Go *allá*!" Let's go there . . . and *allá* we go.

You walk ahead, your bare butt already covered in sand from a couple of falls on the dune. The beach lies smooth, flat, and glistening with fresh, wet shells after the low tide. I point at the rising sun over the water and you clap again calling "Lu!" for *luna*, moon. "Yes, Loretta, *la luna* looks like the sun," and at my words you touch the mole on my right cheek you particularly like and say "Lu!" again for *lunar*, mole. You turn away, rushing toward the sea, looking back, taunting me to chase you. I catch you just as you're about to jump into a wave. You run away from me again staring up at the sky and then you find it, the moon, and squeal with joy. "Lu, lu, lu!!" you call out to me, pointing your whole twenty-three-pound body upward until you're standing on your toes, both arms reaching up to the sky.

I applaud and you run to me with your arms outstretched, seeking a hug, a hug that feels like a dip in the ocean, a baptism, a rebirth. I hug you tight, thinking you're already sixteen months old. The coral heads are showing glittering pools in between them. It will be a full moon soon and the low tides are at their lowest. I take you to the pools. In the shallows are white sand dollars en-

graved in the powdery sand. You jump excitedly in the glistening water. We walk back to our small front porch. I sit down;
you climb up to my lap and begin nursing. With legs in the sun
we laugh and nurse and laugh again. At times your whole face is
still, grows quiet, your eyes wet, your cheeks flushed a pale red,
and I know it is the rush of milk filling you, warming all of your
little life.

NOVEMBER 28, FRIDAY · As I write this the thought of
the future spins through me. My mind flashes to the thousand
chances that converged to recreate my life. I look out the window
and take in the expanse of an ocean coming to a halt at the coral
heads on the beach. You are nineteen months old and I am pregnant again. The due date is August 7, 2006, my thirty-seventh
birthday.

Your inevitable growth and independence from me is a constant
reminder that I am ultimately alone, that melting into another,
the stuff of my personal biography, won't solve a thing. Once, in
the womb, we seemed to be one.

The wish for fusion is the deep desire to resist the loss that the
passage of time implies.

Already a second pregnancy at times feels like a farewell. But
I'm growing less terrified of change and growth. You will grow up,
leave my breast, stop staring into my eyes with that piercing absolute love, and so will follow the child now in my womb.

I have written this version of my life hoping my future lives are
less inauthentic. I know that there are no perfect lives. I have given
up on that childhood fantasy of making myself over through giant,
epic leaps, of starting over every morning to make it all right. The
"right" life does not exist, will forever elude me. A perfect day

with my daughter, for example, today, right now, is all I have, a quiet evening with my husband reading each other, reading others, laughing at ourselves and at the world. And what more could one possibly want?

DECEMBER 24, MONDAY • Tonight, after I put you down to sleep, I returned to the room and stood by the crib. It anguished me to realize for the first time: "I will die and have to leave you." It also occurred to me that one day not in the distant future, you would stand by a crib watching your own child asleep, realizing the same thing. I grew calmer. The calm, as always seems to be the case with me, was made of resignation. But no matter how painful, I look forward to watching you grow, to hearing the sound of your voice change, all linking the woman I am to the child I once was.

Loretta Mae. You are the bond between me and the world I come from. You are becoming my origins.